PENGUIN CLASSICS

THE HOMERIC HYMNS

JULES CASHFORD was originally a classicist who came back to the *Homeric Hymns* through myth and literature, as poems in their own right. Her publications include *The Moon: Myth and Image* (2003), *The Myth of Isis and Osiris*, *Theseus and the Minotaur* and, with Anne Baring, *The Myth of the Goddess: Evolution of an Image*.

NICHOLAS RICHARDSON was educated at Winchester and Magdalen College, Oxford. Since 1968 he has been a Fellow and Tutor in Classics at Merton College, Oxford. His publications include editions of the *Homeric Hymn to Demeter* and books 21–4 of Homer's *Iliad*.

The Homeric Hymns

Translated by JULES CASHFORD
with an Introduction and Notes by
NICHOLAS RICHARDSON

PENGUIN BOOKS

PENGUIN BOOKS

Published by the Penguin Group
Penguin Books Ltd, 80 Strand, London WC2R ORL, England
Penguin Putnam Inc., 375 Hudson Street, New York, New York 10014, USA
Penguin Books Australia Ltd, 250 Camberwell Road, Camberwell, Victoria 3124, Australia
Penguin Books Canada Ltd, 10 Alcorn Avenue, Toronto, Ontario, Canada M4V 3B2
Penguin Books India (P) Ltd, 11, Community Centre, Panchsheel Park, New Delhi – 110 017, India
Penguin Books (NZ) Ltd, Cnr Rosedale and Airborne Roads, Albany, Auckland, New Zealand
Penguin Books (South Africa) (Pty) Ltd, 24 Sturdee Avenue, Rosebank 2196, South Africa

Penguin Books Ltd, Registered Offices: 80 Strand, London WC2R ORL, England

www.penguin.com

First published 2003

021

Translation copyright © Jules Cashford, 2003
Introduction and Notes copyright © Nicholas Richardson, 2003
All rights reserved

The moral rights of the editors have been asserted

Set in 10.25/12.25 pt PostScript Adobe Sabon
Typeset by Rowland Phototypesetting Ltd, Bury St Edmunds, Suffolk
Printed in England by Clays Ltd, St Ives plc

ISBN-13: 978-0-140-43782-9

www.greenpenguin.co.uk

Penguin Books is committed to a sustainable
future for our business, our readers and our planet.
This book is made from Forest Stewardship
Council™ certified paper.

Contents

The Homeric Hymns

Introduction

THE NATURE AND PURPOSE OF
THE HOMERIC HYMNS

The hymns are a group of thirty-three songs composed to honour the gods and goddesses of the ancient Greek pantheon. They are called 'Homeric' because it was often assumed in antiquity that they were composed by Homer, the poet to whom the epics called the *Iliad* and *Odyssey* were attributed. European literature has its origins in these two monumental works. The Greeks and Romans believed that Homer was the greatest of ancient poets, and the fact that the hymns were also attributed to him is a tribute to their high quality. Thus, for instance, the Greek historian Thucydides has no hesitation in quoting the 'Hymn to Apollo' as Homer's work (3.104).

The hymns are composed in the same metre as that of the Homeric epics. This is known as the hexameter, because it consists of six metrical units or feet, each of which is either a dactyl (a long and two short syllables) or a spondee (two long syllables). The interplay of these two metrical lengths gives great variety and flexibility to hexameter verse. In the centuries preceding the composition of the *Iliad* and *Odyssey* a very elaborate tradition had evolved as the ideal medium for composition of epic verse, i.e. poetry in praise of both the great men of the legendary past (the heroes) and the gods who were thought to govern the universe. This traditional means of expression was also the basis for the composition of the hymns, and that is why they are said to be 'Homeric' in style.

The other major composer of early Greek hexameter poetry was Hesiod. He was the author of the *Theogony*, which describes the origins and genealogy of the gods, and how Zeus came to be in control of the world, and the *Works and Days*, a didactic poem about justice, which also contains practical advice on farming, commerce by sea and other subjects. There were other poems attributed to Hesiod, most of which do not survive, except for quotations and fragments on papyri. In addition, we know of a range of other lost epic poems, from quotations and fragments, which made up a body of mythical material and filled in the background to the major Homeric and Hesiodic works.

It is against this literary setting that we should view the hymns. The picture they present of the gods and of their interaction with men is broadly similar to that of these other works, and some of the stories they tell are also mentioned in the Homeric or Hesiodic poems (for example, the rape of Persephone, or the love of Aphrodite for Anchises and the birth of their son Aeneas).

The hymns vary considerably in length. The briefest of them (XIII, to Demeter) is only three lines, the longest (IV, to Hermes) consists of 580 lines. They are sometimes referred to in antiquity as 'preludes' (*prooimia*), as for example by Thucydides, when he quotes parts of the 'Hymn to Apollo'. Many of them end with a formulaic verse in which the poet says that he will go on to sing another song, and two (XXXI, to Helios and XXXII, to Selene) declare that he will sing next of the famous deeds of the race of demigods, i.e. heroic epic narrative. This suggests that hymns of this kind were (at least originally) designed as introductions to longer narrative poems. A singer would begin by invoking and praising a god (whichever one was appropriate to the particular occasion of recitation), or by singing a series of hymns to different deities, before going on to sing a more extensive epic song.

The fifth-century poet Pindar tells us that the Homeridae (a guild of singers who claimed to be descendants or followers of Homer) usually began their recitations 'with a prelude to Zeus' (*Nemean Ode* 2), and in the *Odyssey* the singer Demodokos, the court-poet of the Phaeacians, begins a song about the Wooden

Horse at Troy 'from the god', i.e. probably with an invocation for divine aid (Odyssey 8.499). The *Iliad* and *Odyssey* both open with a brief invocation of the Muse, asking her to tell the tale which is to follow, but in Hesiod's *Theogony* this motif is developed into what is virtually a hymn in praise of the Muses, describing their birth and nature, which occupies the first 115 lines of this poem, and the opening verses of the *Works and Days* (1–8) are a shorter hymn in praise of Zeus.

We can glimpse something similar in the splendid scene in the 'Hymn to Apollo', in which the poet describes the festival of Apollo on the island of Delos (III, 146–64). He praises the wonderful skill of the Delian girls who are the attendants of the god:

> first they sing to Apollo, then to Leto
> and to Artemis who delights in arrows,
>
> and then they sing a song recalling
> the men and women who lived long ago,
> and so they enchant the tribes of human beings.
>
> (158–61)

Once again we hear of hymns to the deities of this festival, followed by song in praise of famous men of the past.

In the case of the shorter Homeric hymns, their role as preludes seems clear enough, but the longer ones contain extensive narratives, and some scholars have doubted whether these would actually have been intended to be followed by other epic recitations. There is really no way of telling whether this was so or not, but in principle there seems no reason why they should not have been designed as genuine preludes, at least when they were first composed.

COMPOSITION AND PERFORMANCE

It is usually believed nowadays that the tradition from which our surviving early Greek epic poetry grew was an 'oral' one, i.e. that singers composed without the aid of writing. Archaeological evidence points to a gap between the twelfth and ninth centuries BC, during which written records have not (at least as yet) been found in Greece or the Greek settlements around the area of the Aegean Sea. Before this time the late Bronze Age cultures of Crete and Greece (known as Minoan and Mycenaean respectively) wrote Greek in a syllabic script (called Linear B), whereas the Greek alphabetic script appears only from the eighth century BC onwards, when the Greeks took over and adapted the script used by the Phoenicians.

The highly formulaic character of much early epic verse is thought to be the result of the evolution during this period of a poetic language which enabled singers to compose or improvise songs, based on the pattern of the traditional ones which they had heard in the past. It remains unclear whether or not the major Homeric and Hesiodic poems which we still possess were composed with the aid of writing. Since these poems are usually thought to date from soon after the introduction of the alphabetic script, and as some of our earliest surviving examples of this script are actually in hexameter verse, it seems likely that the development of alphabetic writing gave an impetus to the composition of poems on a much larger scale than had previously been normal. For without the possibility of some form of written record, it is unlikely that works as large as the *Iliad* and *Odyssey* could have survived in transmission without suffering extensive changes.

This does not necessarily mean that Homer himself was able to write down his own compositions. An ancient tradition held that he was blind, and, if this is true, he cannot have done so. But he could have dictated them, or they could have been memorized and recorded by pupils later (such as the so-called Homeridae). The poet of the 'Hymn to Apollo' identifies himself as a blind man, who lives in the rocky island of Chios (III, 172). Whether or not this means that he is Homer himself, at least we can say of him (if he is speaking the truth) that he was an 'oral' poet, i.e. one who composed and recited without using a text.

Most early Greek poetry, whether written down or not, was intended, at least primarily, to be heard rather than read. In the case of the Homeric hymns, it seems likely that they were composed for recitation at festivals, such as the one in Delos described in the 'Hymn to Apollo', of which the poet says:

> But, Phoebus, it is Delos
> that most delights your heart. There for your sake
> the Ionians gather in their trailing robes
>
> with their children and their revered wives.
> There they delight you with boxing and dancing
> and song, remembering you
>
> whenever they hold their festivals. (III, 146–50)

After praising the Delian girls, the poet goes on to ask them to sing his praise in return, saying:

> Remember me in the time to come,
>
> whenever someone on this earth
> – a stranger who has suffered many things –
> arrives here and asks you:
>
> 'Girls,
> who is the sweetest man of all the singers
> who comes here to you,
>
> who is it most delights you?'
> Answer him together, all of you,
> with one voice:
>
> 'The blind man who lives in rocky Chios,
> all his songs will be the best,
> now and in the time to come.' (III, 166–73)

Since these Greek festivals included contests in singing, this looks very much like a plea for victory in the contest on Delos. Another hymn (VI, to Aphrodite) closes with a prayer to the goddess for 'victory in this contest', and several of them end by asking the deity to grant favour or honour to the poet's song (X, to Aphrodite, XXIV, to Hestia; XXV, to the Muses and Apollo).

We do not know a great deal about the musical aspects of early epic performance. Homer describes singers accompanying their song with a stringed instrument (*kitharis* or *phorminx*). When Hermes has invented the lyre in the 'Hymn to Hermes', he uses it to sing a hymn about his own birth, and later he demonstrates his skill to Apollo by singing about the origins of the gods in general, to its accompaniment (IV, 57–61, 425–33). In the 'Hymn to Apollo', Apollo himself accompanies with his *kitharis* the songs and dances of the Muses and other gods, and later he again plays his *phorminx* as he leads his Cretan priests, while they sing a paean in his honour (III, 182–93, 514–19).

It seems, however, that at some stage the performance of epic song changed to a form of recitation accompanied by a staff, which the performer used to emphasize his words, like the staff or sceptre used by orators in Homer's poems. Hesiod already speaks of himself as having been given a staff by the Muses, when he received from them his gift of song (*Theogony* 30–32).

AUTHORSHIP AND DATES OF COMPOSITION

Even in ancient times, some later writers (e.g. Athenaeus, who wrote *c.* AD 200, and a few others) expressed doubts about whether the hymns were really the work of Homer. Modern scholars have tended to date most of them to the 'Archaic' period of Greek literature (i.e. the seventh and sixth centuries BC), and to regard them as the work of a range of different poets. The 'Hymn to Apollo' is the only one in which the poet gives us any information about himself, and even here he does not tell us his name. The tradition about Homer's blindness could well be due to the belief that this hymn is Homer's work. This tradition is first attested to by Thucydides, and is a standard feature of the later accounts of Homer's life. But it is also theoretically possible that some or all of this hymn really *is* the work of Homer (as Thucydides believed). There is, however, another ancient tradition (recorded later by a commentator on Pindar's second Nemean ode), which ascribes this poem to one of the Homeridae, named Kynaithos of Chios, and appears to date his work to the late sixth century BC. David Ruhnken suggested in 1782 that this poem was originally two separate hymns, the first describing Apollo's birth on Delos and the festival there (lines 1–178), the second his foundation of the Delphic oracle. Since then scholars have argued about this question. What seems clear is that the second (or so-called 'Pythian') part is very closely related to the first (or 'Delian') part, since it echoes many of its themes. Whatever the original circumstances of composition, the hymn as we have it is evidently intended to be treated as a single work, and that is how we should read it today.

The hymn ends with a warning to Apollo's new priests at Delphi, that if they act unjustly they will have to accept others as their masters (III, 538–44). This looks as if it could be a 'prophecy after the event'. There was a tradition that control of the Delphic sanctuary was taken over early in the sixth century BC by a group of northern Greek states under the leadership of Thessaly (the Amphictionic League), after a war with the local people of Krisa, and some scholars have thought that the hymn must allude to this event. If so, the poem as we have it would be later than this date. But it has also been argued that the reference in the hymn has nothing to do with the tradition about the war, and this question still remains open.

Attempts have also been made to date the hymns by using various criteria of style and language. The most recent systematic study of this kind puts the longer hymns (II–V) within the Archaic period, the oldest one being the 'Hymn to Aphrodite' (early seventh century) and the latest the 'Hymn to Hermes' (late sixth century).[1] But the evidence is not really sufficient to reach definite conclusions. A few of the shorter hymns (e.g. XXXI and XXXII, Helios and Selene respectively) could be later, and one (VIII, to Ares) clearly did not originally belong in this collection. Its style and language suggest that it was composed in late antiquity. Proclus, the fifth-century AD Neoplatonist, who wrote a collection of hymns which we still possess, has been suggested as a candidate for authorship, but this too remains uncertain.

STRUCTURE AND THEMES

The shortest hymn (XIII, to Demeter) consists of two lines announcing its subject, Demeter and her daughter Persephone, and a closing verse asking Demeter to 'save our city and guide my song'. The two goddesses are briefly characterized by epithets of praise, and that is all. The other short hymns add more information about the deity, usually by means of a relative clause, describing their parentage and birth, their upbringing, or their typical activities and effect on mankind. Nearly all end with a closing verse or verses, invoking the god, and often asking for divine favour. Hymn XII, to Hera, is exceptional in not having any closing formula of invocation. Hymn VIII, to Ares, ends with a prayer, but no expression of farewell. Many, as we have already seen, announce at the end that another song will follow.

This simple and basic structure forms a framework within which a longer narrative can be developed, based on a range of possible themes. Clearly the god's birth is a major event which can be celebrated in more or less detail. Quite often it is complicated, involving concealment or hostility (as in the case of children of Zeus by wives other than Hera, such as Apollo, Hermes, the Dioskouroi, etc.) Sometimes it is an event with dramatic and cosmic repercussions: the extraordinary birth of Athena, fully armed, from the head of Zeus, has a powerful effect on the whole universe (XXVIII, to Athena), and when Apollo is born the attendant goddesses utter a loud cry, and the island of Delos responds to his epiphany by covering herself in golden flowers (III, 119, 135–9).

This theme of the impact created by a new god's appearance is naturally linked to that of his introduction to the company of the other gods on Olympos, and his reception as a member of the pantheon, or divine family. This can follow directly on his birth, as in the case of Pan: his birth is celebrated in a miniature hymn by the nymphs within hymn XIX, and he is introduced to the gods by his father Hermes soon after his arrival. But it can occur in other contexts, too. The brief hymn to Herakles (XV) describes his birth and Labours on behalf of mankind, and then tells how he now lives with Hebe (goddess of youth) on Olympos, as a reward for his life of heroic exploits. Apollo's entry to Olympos is dramatically set at the very beginning of his hymn: he appears in Zeus' palace as an archer with his bow drawn, and this causes consternation among the gods, until the tension is defused by his mother Leto, who unstrings his bow and leads him to a seat. This scene introduces the theme of the god's birth, as Leto is said to be full of joy because she has produced so mighty a son, and the actual narrative of Apollo's birth follows soon after.

The same scene is mirrored at the opening of the second part of this hymn, where Apollo is portrayed as the god of music, going up to Olympos from Delphi and leading the gods in song and dancing (III, 182–206).

In the 'Hymn to Hermes' (IV), the god's birth is immediately followed by various exploits while he is still a baby, of which the greatest is his theft of his brother Apollo's cattle. When Apollo has tracked him down, he takes him up to heaven, to accuse him of the crime before their father Zeus, and Zeus as arbiter reconciles the pair (322–96). His introduction to the gods thus takes a particular form here, as part of a larger narrative. After the cattle have been recovered, both gods again return to Olympos and are welcomed there.

In the 'Hymn to Demeter' (XIII) Persephone is picking flowers on earth when Hades carries her off, but Demeter takes revenge by leaving the company of the gods and creating a famine on earth. It is only when Persephone has been brought back by Hermes that both goddesses are said to go up to Olympos and live there with the other gods, although Persephone must still spend one third of the year with her husband in the Underworld.

In some of the other hymns, the motif of the nursing or upbringing of the deity naturally follows that of his birth. In hymn VI, Aphrodite's birth is not actually described, but it is implied by the brief reference to how the foam of the sea (in which she was born) carried her to Cyprus, where the Seasons (Horai) welcomed her, and then an elaborate description follows of how they dress her and adorn her with jewellery. When this is done they introduce her to the other gods, who greet her, wonder at her beauty and pray to marry her. In hymn XXVI Dionysos is nursed by the nymphs in the glens of Nysa and grows up in a sweet-smelling cavern. Then he roams through the woodland glades, accompanied by the nymphs. In the 'Hymn to Apollo', after Apollo's birth he is fed on nectar and ambrosia by Themis (goddess of right), and at once breaks free of the baby clothes in which he is wrapped.

Divine nurture, however, and entry to heaven are normally counterbalanced by some description of a god's interaction with mankind. The Greek gods needed the worship and offerings of mortals, if not for their physical survival then at least for their prestige and honour. When Demeter creates a famine on earth, the gods are threatened with the loss of their sacrifices, and this forces Zeus to intervene and send Hermes to rescue Demeter's daughter from Hades. Many of the hymns speak of the god's favourite sanctuaries and the honours which men give them. In hymn IX, Artemis goes through Smyrna to Klaros, in order to join Apollo: Klaros was one of the major centres of Apollo's cult in Asia Minor. In hymn X, Aphrodite is hailed as ruler over Salamis and Cyprus, and Poseidon is the lord of Helikon and Aigai in hymn XXII. In hymn XXVII, Artemis visits her brother's temple at Delphi. At the end of the 'Hymn to Demeter' she and Persephone are addressed as the goddesses of Eleusis, Paros and Antron in Thessaly.

Some of the major hymns take this basic theme a stage further, because they actually tell the story of how the god's cult was first instituted. The 'Hymn to Demeter' (II) recounts in detail how the goddess's search for her daughter brought her to Eleusis, disguised as an old woman. Here she is received by Metaneira, the wife of Keleos, king of Eleusis, and becomes nurse to their baby son Demophoon. When her attempt to make him immortal fails, she reveals her identity and orders the people of Eleusis to build her a temple and altar. She stays in the temple until Persephone has returned to earth, and then teaches the Eleusinian leaders her secret rites (the 'Eleusinian Mysteries'), which are said to offer initiates a better fate after death.

Thus this hymn claims for Eleusis a special status as the leading centre for the cult of Demeter and Persephone, and this suggests that it could have been designed as propaganda on behalf of Eleusis, which certainly later claimed to be the most important sanctuary for Demeter's secret rites.

In the first part of the 'Hymn to Apollo' Leto promises Delos that Apollo will build his first temple on the island, and Delos is said to be his favourite place of worship. The second part is concerned with Apollo's search for a site for his oracle, which culminates in his choice of Pytho (the later Delphi). He then commandeers a ship containing Cretan merchants and takes them to Pytho, where he tells them that they will become his first Delphic priests.

The 'Hymn to Hermes' is mainly about Hermes' theft of Apollo's cattle, but when he has driven them to the river Alpheios (in the north-west Peloponnese, near Olympia), he slaughters two of them and divides the meat into twelve portions. Later it was customary to sacrifice to a group of twelve Olympian deities, and it looks as if this episode may be intended to mark the origin of this practice.

No cult is actually established in the longer 'Hymn to Aphrodite' (V), but when Aphrodite first appears to Anchises, disguised as a beautiful young girl, his immediate reaction is to assume that she must really be a goddess and to promise to set up an altar to her and offer regular sacrifices; he adds a prayer for favour for himself and his children in the future.

This shows how closely the theme of a god's worship (prayer and sacrifice) is linked to that of his appearance to men, or his 'epiphany'. In some cases, the god appears in disguise, but this event is still powerful enough to evoke reactions of religious awe and fear. In hymn II, when Demeter sets foot on the threshold of the palace at Eleusis, suddenly her head touches the roof-beam and she fills the doorway with divine radiance. Metaneira is immediately seized by awe, reverence and pale terror. In the scene which follows we have the description of a sequence of actions which are designed to account for the origin of some parts of the preliminary rituals of the Eleusinian Mysteries, when the person to be initiated had to sit on a special stool covered with a fleece, with his head veiled, in a rite of purification, and he would break a period of fasting by drinking a specially prepared mixture of barley, mint and water, called a *kykeon* (191–211). In the same scene Demeter is also persuaded to laugh and ease her grief by a servant called Iambe, and again this can be seen as the mythical model for the practice of ritual jesting or abuse in the cult of Eleusis.

This scene shows how the partial or preliminary revelation of the goddess is associated with the institution of various aspects of her cult. In the same way, her fuller epiphany, or self-revelation, later is accompanied by the command to set up her sanctuary, and her promise that she will teach the Eleusinians her Mysteries (268–74).

The Greeks used the word *aition* to mean the origin or cause of something, and aetiology is the term sometimes used to describe this process whereby the origin of particular customs or rituals (etc.) is explained by stories or myths. Some of the hymns are clearly aetiological in this sense. Not only do they chart the institution of certain cults and rituals, but in some cases they also account for the invention of other aspects of human culture. The 'Hymn to Hermes' (IV) is particularly rich in this respect, since it describes Hermes' invention of the lyre, which he creates from a tortoiseshell (39–51), and his discovery of the art of kindling fire with firesticks (108–14), as well as his twelve-part sacrifice. (The hides of the cattle are said to be 'even now, after so many years, ... still there', i.e. the relics of this event were on display.) After the reconciliation of Hermes and Apollo they exchange gifts: Hermes gives his brother the lyre, Apollo gives him his goad and puts him in charge of cattle. Hermes then invents the shepherd's pipes (*syrinx*), and Apollo gives him his golden wand, and a special type of prophecy at Delphi. He is also made the lord of wild and tame beasts in general, and the messenger to the Underworld. The whole poem of course also accounts for his role as the god of theft and deception.

In the longer 'Hymn to Aphrodite' (V), the goddess tells Anchises how their union will lead to the birth of Aeneas, who will rule over the Trojans, and whose descendants will continue in future generations (196–99). A similar prophecy occurs in the *Iliad* (20.307–8). Later Greek traditions held that the ruling family, either in Troy itself or in a place near Troy called Skepsis, was descended from Aeneas. It has been suggested therefore that the hymn was composed in order to honour this dynasty and account for its origins. We cannot be sure that this is true, but it seems a reasonable possibility.

The hymns, then, tell us something about the Greek view of the relationship between the divine and human worlds, which complements what the Homeric and Hesiodic poems have to say. In some cases, such as those of Herakles or Aeneas, the actual union of a deity with a mortal produces an exceptional human being: this was the origin of some of the greatest of the heroes in the *Iliad*, such as Achilles or Sarpedon, and this mixing of the divine and the human gives rise to the race of heroes as a whole, whose genealogies were described in poetry attributed to Hesiod.

Apart from this, individual men do not play a very prominent part in the hymns. The 'Hymn to Demeter' (II) is exceptional, in naming the rulers at Eleusis and the family of Keleos, but elsewhere they are often unnamed, like the Cretan priests of Apollo, or the old man of Onchestos who is the only witness of Hermes' theft, or the pirates in the 'Hymn to Dionysos' (VII). On the other hand, these poems do give us a more general view of men's situation in relation to the gods, and they emphasize the gulf which exists between these two worlds in various ways, as well as their interaction. Demeter, for example, fails in her attempt to immortalize the infant Demophoon because of human folly, the fatal curiosity of his mother, who watches at night to see what she is doing (242–5). Demophoon will therefore have to die, although he will be commemorated in an annual festival. However, she is able to bestow on mankind in general the gift of her Mysteries. The favour of Demeter and Persephone can bring one prosperity in one's lifetime, and, although it cannot rescue men from death, it offers the promise of a better afterlife (480–83).

Demeter, when detected by Metaneira, laments the ignorance and helplessness of men:

> 'How ignorant are human beings, how mindless they are,
> not to foresee the destiny that is coming towards them,
> not to know whether it is good or whether it is bad.' (256–7)

This motif is echoed by the Muses' song in the 'Hymn to Apollo'.

> they sing of the divine gifts of the gods
> and of the sufferings of human beings
> which the gods bring upon them,
> how they live, mindless, helpless,
> how they can't find a cure for death,
> can't stop old age. (190–93)

Ignorance of the future, the uncertainty of life and above all the inevitable nature of old age and death, are recurrent themes of early Greek literature. These are the things which separate men from the gods, who are ageless and deathless and can live a life of ease. The 'Hymn to Aphrodite' (V), which praises Aphrodite's power in mixing gods with mortals (34–41), also reflects upon the limits of mortality. Aphrodite says that Anchises' family was always close to the gods, and she gives the examples of Ganymede and Tithonos. The former was carried off by Zeus because of his beauty to be the cupbearer of the gods, to live with them for ever, ageless and immortal. But Tithonos was less lucky: his lover Dawn asked the gods for immortality for him, but forgot to ask them to give him eternal youth; when he grew old she could bear him no longer but shut him away out of sight. Aphrodite predicts that Anchises will not escape old age either, and so she would not want him to be immortal (239–46). Even the mountain nymphs, to whom she will entrust the child Aeneas, and whose nature is between those of gods and mortal men, will eventually die, because their lives are bound up with those of the great pines and oaks in their mountain homes (257–72).

In these various ways the boundaries of mortality are explored by these poems, as well as the nature of the gods themselves.

STYLE AND POETIC QUALITY

The hymns are delightful poems, full of life and charm. They exemplify the quality of beauty which the Greeks called *charis* (grace). In this respect they resemble early Greek lyric poetry. They have a richness of ornamental detail which is sometimes found in the longer Homeric epics, but the style of these is usually plainer. At the same time the major hymns use many of the narrative techniques of Homeric epic, although on a smaller scale.

The gods of Homer can be both awe-inspiring and comic. In the *Iliad* we have scenes of sublime grandeur, portraying their power and majesty, as well as episodes where some of them can seem all too fallible and petty, even ridiculous. In the *Odyssey* they are usually more dignified, but here too we have the delight-ful, light-hearted song of Demodokos to the Phaeacians about the adultery of Ares and Aphrodite, and how Aphrodite's hus-band Hephaistos took his revenge on them (8.266–366). The hymns, too, can be both serious and comic. The story of Deme-ter's loss of her daughter reflects the breathtaking solemnity of these goddesses, who have power over the gifts of the earth and over life after death. Apollo's abrupt first entry to Olympos reveals his dangerous character, which also makes Delos tremble at the prospect of receiving him (III, 1–4, 62–82), just as we see him at the opening of the *Iliad* sending plague on the Greek army with his deadly arrows. But he is also shown as the god of music and of the festival, on Delos, at Delphi, and on Olympos, just as he leads the Muses in song at the close of book 1 of the *Iliad*. The gravity and sorrow of Demeter too is counter-balanced by the lovely picture of Persephone picking flowers with the daughters of Okeanos at the opening of her hymn, or the graceful beauty of the daughters of Keleos who receive her and bring her to the palace of Eleusis, or the jesting of Iambe.

In contrast to the general seriousness of these two hymns, the one to Hermes is almost entirely comic, mirroring the quicksilver brilliance of this god of tricks. Hermes' practical inventiveness is equalled by his rhetorical skill: not only does he literally cover his tracks, but he also knows how to claim innocence without actually perjuring himself (73–86, 368–86). It is typical of him that, when Apollo picks him up in order to carry him off to Zeus, Hermes lets off

> an omen, an insolent servant
> of the belly – a presumptuous messenger –
> and immediately after this he sneezed

so that Apollo drops him at once. Hermes' fart is described with a mock-solemn, riddling periphrasis: it suits his character as a baby and completely undermines Apollo's threats (294–300).

The 'Hymn to Aphrodite' (V) has serious undertones, as it alludes to the risks involved in such encounters between men and goddesses (185–90, 200–238, 286–90). But it is filled with irony too. Aphrodite becomes her own victim, and Zeus takes revenge for all the confusion she has sowed in the past. Like Hermes she is a mistress of the arts of deception. Anchises glimpses the truth, but allows himself to believe her story, and cannot wait for the marriage she has proposed. Afterwards comes the bitter awakening, with shame and recrimination and fear of the consequences for him. She swears him to secrecy with a dire warning in case he disobeys, but we suspect that (as in later tradition) he could not keep the truth to himself and suffered as a result.

In its celebration of both the irresistible power and the weakness of the goddess of love this hymn resembles those semicomic episodes in the Homeric epics where divine amours are portrayed, such as the Deception of Zeus by Hera in the *Iliad* (book 14) or the song of Ares and Aphrodite in the *Odyssey* (book 8).

The shorter hymns too have this mixture of charm and solemnity. Dionysos (always an ambiguous deity) is captured by pirates, who ignore their helmsman's warning that he is a god.

But their ropes will not hold him, wine bubbles up in their ship and it is covered in vine clusters and ivy. The god becomes a roaring lion, a bear suddenly appears too, and then the pirates leap overboard and become dolphins. Only the helmsman is saved.

This somewhat bizarre sequence has an ebullience of life and humour which is typical of this god, giver of joy and hilarity, but also dangerous to those who oppose him. (There is a famous sixth-century BC vase-painting by Exekias which catches the spirit of this hymn: it shows Dionysos reclining in a boat and holding a drinking-horn, beneath two vines which climb the mast, and whose grape clusters hang above him, while dolphins sport around him – see cover of this edition.)

The 'Hymn to Pan' (XIX) is also a vivid and humorous portrayal of this restless, ubiquitous god of nature, who roams ceaselessly with the nymphs through the woods and mountains, which echo with their song. His monstrous appearance so terrifies his mother at his birth that she runs away: but Hermes takes him to Olympos, where all the gods are delighted by him.

The 'Hymn to Athena' (XXVIII) has an almost baroque grandeur in its description of her birth, which evokes cosmic awe and terror: but here too at the end 'Wise Zeus was delighted'.

This sense of delight and joy runs through the hymns. Their richness of language evokes the rich beauty of the natural world, of whose power and splendour the Greek gods are the manifestation. This is why these poems from a distant, pagan past continue to speak to us still with so clear a voice even today.

INFLUENCE

In general

The hymns are not often quoted in antiquity, but their influence can be detected in many later classical authors. The 'Hymn to Demeter' (II), for example, was frequently echoed or imitated, especially by the Hellenistic poets (in the third and second centuries BC). The greatest poet of this period, Callimachus,

wrote a collection of hymns which owes a strong debt to the
Homeric hymns in general, and particularly to those for Demeter
and Apollo. Ovid tells the story of the Rape of Persephone twice
(*Metamorphoses* 5.341 ff., *Fasti* 4.417 ff.), echoing both the
Demeter and Aphrodite hymns, and Claudian's *De Raptu
Proserpinae* probably owes something to the Homeric version
of Persephone's rape.

The early lyric poet Alcaeus (*c.* 600 BC) composed a 'hymn
to Hermes', which was clearly close in its theme to the Homeric
one, and was probably influenced either by our hymn or an
earlier epic version of the story. His hymns to Dionysos and
the Dioskouroi were also influenced by hymns in our collection
(I, XXXIII). The Homeric 'Hymn to Hermes' certainly inspired
Sophocles' satyr-play *Ichneutai* (which in turn inspired Tony
Harrison's modern version, *The Trackers*).

Apart from a handful of ancient papyri, the hymns have
reached us through a number of manuscripts of the fourteenth
to sixteenth centuries AD. Giovanni Aurispa, who was respon-
sible for bringing many Greek manuscripts to Italy from the
East, mentions in a letter written in 1424 that he possesses
one which contains the Homeric hymns. It is possible, but not
certain, that this was the archetype from which many of our
manuscripts of the hymns were drawn.[2] The hymns were first
printed at Florence in 1488, together with the *Iliad* and *Odyssey*.
The editor was Demetrios Chalcondyles.

In the later fifteenth century the Italian poet and scholar
Politian certainly knew and used the hymns, and Botticelli seems
to have been inspired by them, through the medium of Politian's
poetry. Thus Botticelli's *Birth of Venus* shows the goddess
blown across the foaming sea by the zephyrs, while one of the
Seasons waits to receive her on land, as in hymn VI.[3]

From the late sixteenth century (*c.* 1570) we have an insight
into how the hymns might be read, in a record made of lectures
by the humanist scholar and poet Jean Dorat, who earlier in his
career had taught some of the leading French poets, including
Ronsard and Du Bellay.[4] Dorat discusses books 10–12 of the
Odyssey, and the opening section (lines 1–32) of the longer
'Hymn to Aphrodite' (V), commenting on the nature of the

goddesses Aphrodite, Athena, Artemis and Hestia. His inter-
pretations are strongly allegorical, as one would expect at this
period, and one can find echoes of his literary views in the poetry
of his pupils.

In the seventeenth century George Chapman was the first to
translate the hymns into English verse, as a sequel to his *Iliad*
and *Odyssey*. His version is in rhyming pentameters, and was
probably published *c.* 1624.[5] Chapman's style is often heavy
and involved, and he adds moralizing comments of his own, but
there are some fine passages.

The story of the love of Aphrodite for Anchises, the subject
of the 'Hymn to Aphrodite', was retold by Phineas Fletcher in a
poem first published in 1628, but probably written between
1600 and 1616, when Fletcher was in Cambridge. But apart
from the basic theme, and the reference at the end to Anchises'
betrayal of his secret and punishment by Jove's thunder, there
is little to connect it with the hymn.[6]

A century later (1710) William Congreve published his trans-
lation of 'Homer's Hymn to Venus'.[7] Congreve was a better
poet and translator than Chapman. Dryden in fact said of him
that he was 'more capable than any man I know' of translating
Homer, and Pope dedicated his *Iliad* to him.[8] Congreve explains
in his Preface to the Reader that he had once thought of translat-
ing the longer hymns to Apollo and Hermes also, but decided
that they were too difficult to understand without a commen-
tary. He speaks of the 'extraordinary pleasure' with which he
had often read them all, and defends the ancient tradition that
they were composed by Homer.

Among the Romantic poets it was Shelley and his circle of
friends who were most attracted by the hymns.[9] Leigh Hunt,
Peacock and Jefferson Hogg all helped to interest Shelley in
them. Leigh Hunt himself composed a rather jaunty version of
the one about Dionysos and the pirates (1814), although Shelley
criticized his style as 'barbarous jargon'.[10] Peacock included a
free adaptation of the same poem in his *Rhododaphne* (1818).[11]
In 1817 Hogg wrote to Shelley about the hymns, calling them
'those miraculous effusions of genius', and Shelley read them
that July. In January 1818 he translated the hymns to Earth,

Sun, Moon, and Castor and Pollux, and the first fifty-five lines of the longer 'Hymn to Aphrodite', in rhyming couplets. He also read Chapman's versions at this time, and echoes him sometimes. In July 1820 he translated the whole of the longer 'Hymn to Hermes', this time in *ottava rima*.[12]

Shelley and his friends were especially attracted by the vitality of the hymns, their more light-hearted aspects and their evocation of the natural world as infused with the divine. Shelley was fascinated by tricky, ethereal spirits (such as Cupid or Ariel), and seems to have felt a special affinity with Mercury. His own son, Percy Florence, was only eight months old when he translated this hymn, and the comic exploits of the infant god must have suited his mood.

Of Shelley's versions John Addington Symonds wrote: 'they have never been surpassed for beauty of form and complete transfusion of the spirit of one literature into the language of another'.[13] One modern critic has called his *Hymn to Mercury* 'one of Shelley's finest achievements', and another considers his versions 'often better than the originals'.[14] Some of his own poems also reflect the hymns, especially *The Witch of Atlas*, which has been described as 'a sort of Homeric hymn, of Shelleyan spirituality, subtlety, and color', and *With a Guitar, to Jane*.[15]

Here is Shelley's *Hymn to Gaia*:

> O Universal Mother, who dost keep
> From everlasting thy foundations deep,
> Eldest of things, Great Earth, I sing of thee!
> All shapes that have their dwelling in the sea,
> All things that fly, or on the ground divine
> Live, move, and there are nourished – these are thine;
> These from thy wealth thou dost sustain; from thee
> Fair babes are born, and fruits on every tree
> Hang ripe and large, revered Divinity!
>
> 10   The life of mortal men beneath thy sway
> Is held; thy power both gives and takes away!
> Happy are they whom thy mild favours nourish;
> All things unstinted round them grow and flourish.

For them, endures the life-sustaining field
Its load of harvest, and their cattle yield
Large increase, and their house with wealth is filled.
Such honoured dwell in cities fair and free,
The homes of lovely women, prosperously;
Their sons exult in youth's new budding gladness,
And their fresh daughters free from care or sadness,   20
With bloom-inwoven dance and happy song,
On the soft flowers the meadow-grass among,
Leap round them sporting – such delights by thee
Are given, rich Power, revered Divinity.

Mother of gods, thou Wife of starry Heaven,
Farewell! be thou propitious, and be given
A happy life for this brief melody,
Nor thou nor other songs shall unremembered be.

From the *Hymn to Mercury* here is Apollo's speech on first
hearing Hermes' lyre ('Hymn to Hermes', 434–62):

These words were wingèd with his swift delight:
    'You heifer-stealing schemer, well do you
Deserve that fifty oxen should requite
    Such minstrelsies as I have heard even now.
Comrade of feasts, little contriving wight,
    One of your secrets I would gladly know,
Whether the glorious power you now show forth
Was folded up within you at your birth,

'Or whether mortal taught or God inspired
    The power of unpremeditated song?
Many divinest sounds have I admired,   10
    The Olympian Gods and mortal men among;
But such a strain of wondrous, strange, untired,
    And soul-awakening music, sweet and strong,
Yet did I never hear except from thee,
Offspring of May, impostor Mercury!

'What Muse, what skill, what unimagined use,
    What exercise of subtlest art, has given
Thy songs such power? – for those who hear may choose
    From three, the choicest of the gifts of Heaven,
20 Delight, and love, and sleep, – sweet sleep, whose dews
    Are sweeter than the balmy tears of even –
And I, who speak this praise, am that Apollo
Whom the Olympian Muses ever follow:

'And their delight is dance, and the blithe noise
    Of song and overflowing poesy;
And sweet, even as desire, the liquid voice
    Of pipes, that fills the clear air thrillingly;
But never did my inmost soul rejoice
    In this dear work of youthful revelry
30 As now. I wonder at thee, son of Jove;
Thy harpings and thy song are soft as love.

'Now since thou hast, although so very small,
    Science of arts so glorious, thus I swear, –
And let this cornel javelin, keen and tall,
    Witness between us what I promise here, –
That I will lead thee to the Olympian Hall,
    Honoured and mighty, with thy mother dear,
And many glorious gifts in joy will give thee,
And even at the end will ne'er deceive thee.'

'Hymn to Demeter'

Up to the late eighteenth century all the known manuscripts of
the hymns were defective, since they lacked the two opening ones
to Dionysos and Demeter. It was only in 1777 that a manuscript
containing the last twelve lines of the Dionysos hymn and the
whole of the one to Demeter was discovered in Moscow. David
Ruhnken first published the 'Hymn to Demeter' in 1780, but
twenty-one verses were omitted, and his first complete edition is
dated 1782. The first English versions were done by Richard Hole
and the Reverend Robert Lucas, both published in 1781.[16]

The story of the Rape of Persephone has always fascinated writers and artists, but until the rediscovery of the Homeric hymn it was the versions of Ovid and Claudian which influenced modern literature.[17] The theme is a popular one in nineteenth- and twentieth-century European poetry. But by no means all of these works appear to be directly indebted to the hymn. For example, the young Swinburne's famous *Hymn to Proserpine* (1866) with its lament for the end of paganism ('Thou hast conquered, O pale Galilean . . .') probably owes more to the German and English Romantics. Both this poem and his *Garden of Proserpine* (1866) are a kind of world-weary celebration of death. *At Eleusis*, however (from the same collection), is closer to the *Homeric Hymn*. It is a long lament by Demeter to the people of Eleusis, in which she tells of her thwarted attempt to immortalize the child of Metaneira. Here, however (as in Ovid's *Fasti* and some other versions), the child is Triptolemos, not Demophoon, and she prophesies at the end that he will become her assistant in giving mankind the arts of agriculture (a standard myth in post-Homeric accounts).[18]

Fresh impetus was given by Walter Pater to interest in the story, with his essay 'The Myth of Demeter and Persephone' (1875–6). Pater gives a synopsis of the Homeric hymn, and goes on to consider the ways in which he thinks the myth may have come into being and developed, and its treatment in later ancient literature and art.[19]

Two poems by George Meredith are based on the story. In *The Day of the Daughter of Hades* (1883) the second part describes the reunion of Demeter and her daughter, although again this diverges from the hymn in setting the scene at Enna in Sicily (as in later Greek and Roman versions). The poem's main theme, however, is a vision of Skiageneia ('Born of Shadow'), the daughter of Persephone and Hades, whom Meredith has invented. But in *The Appeasement of Demeter* (1887) Meredith follows quite closely the episode in the hymn (192–205) where Iambe makes Demeter laugh. In this poem Iambe summons a horse and a mare, amidst general barrenness and gloom, Demeter touches them and they revive, she laughs and all things return to life and love.[20]

In the same year Tennyson wrote his *Demeter and Persephone*, a fine poem which he dedicated to the great classical scholar R. C. Jebb. Tennyson took his inspiration for this directly from the hymn, together with Ovid and Claudian (whose *De Raptu Proserpine* he had translated as a young man). With its more positive tone his poem has been seen as a reply to Swinburne's *Hymn to Proserpine*. Tennyson himself called it 'an antique', but with 'a frame – something modern about it'. The poem is a long speech by Demeter, addressed to her daughter. It closes with the vision of a better future, when there will be 'younger, kindlier Gods',

> Gods indeed,
> To send the noon into the night, and break
> The sunless halls of Hades into Heaven,

and Persephone will

> ... also, reap with me,
> Earth-mother, in the harvest hymn of Earth
> The worship which is Love, and see no more
> The Stone, the Wheel, the dimly-glimmering lawns
> Of that Elysium, all the hateful fires
> Of torment, and the shadowy warriors glide
> Along the silent fields of Asphodel.[21]

Tennyson's most famous poem inspired by the hymns, however, is his *Tithonus* (published 1860, but based on a much earlier version). Inspired ultimately by the story first told in the 'Hymn to Aphrodite' (V, 218–38), it is a meditation by Tithonos himself on his state of utter wretchedness, consumed by 'cruel immortality', and longing for an end to life.[22]

Closest of all modern re-enactments of the 'Hymn to Demeter' (II) is Robert Bridges' *Demeter – A Mask* (1904–5).[23] This classical verse-play dramatizes the story of Persephone's rape and return, with minor variations, and includes the nursing of Demophoon at Eleusis. Demeter acquires sympathy for mankind in general through her care for him, and after failing to immortalize him she realizes that it is no use rescuing only one mortal from death. In the end Persephone's negative vision of death and evil is counterbalanced by Demeter's vision of light and goodness, which her Mysteries will offer to mankind, and the play ends in hope:

> (DEMETER)   ...   And I know
> The power of evil is no power at all
> Against eternal good. 'Tis fire on water,
> As darkness against sunlight, like a dream
> To waken'd will. Foolish was I to fear
> That aught could hurt thee, Cora ... (1067–72)[24]

André Gide's beautiful opera *Perséphone* (1934), with music by Stravinsky, is a development from his earlier, fragmentary version, *Proserpine* (1912). Both were inspired by the hymn, which Gide greatly admired.[25] In *Perséphone* the prologue to each of the three scenes (or *tableaux*) explicitly alludes to Homer's version, but Gide has made some significant changes. Persephone willingly accepts her destiny as queen of the shades, out of pity for their distress, and love for them. She is like a saviour-figure, descending to the Underworld again at the end of the opera to alleviate their sufferings, which seem to be equated with the sufferings of humanity as a whole on this earth:

> Et je veux pas à pas et degré par degré
> Descendre jusqu'au fond de la détresse humaine.

Her return to earth is brought about by the labours of Triptolemos, who is equated with Demeter's nursling Demophoon, and whom Persephone will marry. The closing verses recall the famous words of St John's Gospel about the grain of wheat which dies in order to be reborn:

> Il faut, pour qu'un printemps renaisse
> Que le grain consente à mourir
> Sous terre, afin qu'il reparaisse
> En moisson d'or pour l'avenir.

Gide also used the episode about Demeter's failed attempt to immortalize Demophoon as the preface to his *Retour de l'U.R.R.S.* (1936), an account of his visit to Russia, and some critics have viewed *Perséphone* as a Communist allegory. But later, in 1946, Gide wrote of his realization that the hopes so falsely offered by Communism could only be truly fulfilled through the message of the Gospel.[26]

Some of these modern interpretations show a kind of spiritualization of the myth of Persephone. A truly remarkable example of this is the brief commentary by the philosopher and mystic Simone Weil, which forms part of a series of writings composed during the Second World War, as a result of her conversion to Christianity.[27] Like some of the early Fathers of the Church, she came to see ancient Greek philosophy and literature as prefiguring the message of the Gospels through divinely inspired insight, and this leads to a series of interpretations which could be viewed as Neoplatonist or Christian allegories. For her they represent the true meaning of the works concerned. Thus she translates parts of the opening scene of the 'Hymn to Demeter' (II, 1–21, 30–31), and the passage where Hades gives Persephone a pomegranate seed to eat, so that she will be bound to return to him (360–74). Persephone is lured by the marvellous beauty of the narcissus into plucking this flower, and at this moment she is seized by Hades. For Simone Weil this represents the soul searching for divine beauty, and being captured by the unseen God through the trap or lure of beauty in earthly things. The pomegranate seed is something tiny in itself, but infinitely significant: this represents the soul's acceptance of God, which is almost unconscious but has infinite consequences. It is like the grain of mustard in Christ's parable, which symbolizes the kingdom of heaven, at first the smallest of grains, but later growing into a mighty tree.

CONCLUSION

From the Renaissance onwards the hymns have been an inspiration to writers, artists and musicians.[28] In the past two centuries there have also been a good many other translations into English and other languages, although none by poets as famous as Congreve or Shelley. Recent scholars have studied the hymns from a variety of different viewpoints: as part of the tradition of early Greek hexameter poetry, as examples of mythical modes of narrative, as documents illustrating Greek views of their gods, or simply because of their special qualities as works of art.

Many questions still remain unsolved, for example about their authorship and dating, methods of composition and contexts of performance. But there is a growing awareness both of their poetic value and also of their significance in the development of archaic Greek religious thought. This translation gives the general reader the opportunity of sharing in the appreciation and enjoyment of their beauty.

NOTES

1. Richard Janko, *Homer, Hesiod and the Hymns* (Cambridge, 1982).
2. Rudolf Pfeiffer, *History of Classical Scholarship 1300–1850* (Oxford, 1976), 48.
3. Edgar Wind, *Pagan Mysteries in the Renaissance* (London, 1958), 110, 113–7; Ronald Lightbown, *Sandro Botticelli: Life and Work* (London, 1989), 159–60.
4. Jean Dorat, *Mythologicum ou interpretation allégorique de l'Odyssée X–XII et de l'Hymne à Aphrodite*, ed. Philip Ford (Geneva, 2000), especially 88–101.
5. George Chapman, *The Crowne of all Homers Workes* (London), reprinted in *Chapman's Homer*, ed. Allardyce Nicoll, vol. 2 (London, 1957), 501–639.
6. *Venus and Anchises (Brittain's Ida) and other Poems by Phineas Fletcher*, ed. Ethel Seaton (Oxford, 1926), 1–20. In Stanza 59,

'He gladly dyes and death new life applying
Gladlie again revives that oft he may be dying'

might possibly be an echo of the 'Hymn to Aphrodite', 153–4, but
given the commonness of this conceit, this seems unlikely.

7. *The Complete Works of William Congreve*, ed. Montague Summers,
vol. 4 (London, 1923), 164–76.

8. *William Congreve, Letters and Documents*, ed. John C. Hodges
(London, 1964), 75, 89–90, 156, 233–4.

9. Timothy Webb, *The Violet in the Crucible: Shelley and Translation*
(Oxford, 1976), especially 51–79.

10. James Leigh Hunt, 'Bacchus, or the Pirates', in *The Feast of the
Poets* (London, 1814), reprinted in *The Poetical Works of Leigh Hunt*,
ed. Humphrey S. Milford (Oxford, 1923), 389–90; Timothy Webb,
The Violet in the Crucible, 60–61.

11. Thomas Love Peacock, *Rhododaphne* (London, 1818), lines
159–202, reprinted in *The Works of Thomas Love Peacock*, vol. 7
(London, 1931), 56–7.

12. *The Complete Poetical Works of Percy Bysshe Shelley*, ed. T.
Hutchinson (Oxford, 1905), 680–704. For a facsimile of the manu-
script of the 1818 versions cf. Nancy M. Goslee (ed.), *Bodleian MS.
Shelley Adds. 12* (New York, 1996). Cf. also Timothy Webb, *The
Violet in the Crucible*, 63–79, 90–141.

13. John Addington Symonds, *Shelley* (London, 1878), 113.

14. Timothy Webb, *The Violet in the Crucible*, 123; Douglas Bush,
Mythology and the Romantic Tradition (Cambridge, Mass., 1937),
138.

15. Douglas Bush, *Mythology and the Romantic Tradition*, 139–43;
Timothy Webb, *The Violet in the Crucible*, 73–4, 77–9.

16. David Ruhnken, *Homeri Hymnus in Cererem* (Leiden, 1780);
Richard H. Hole, *Homer's Hymn to Ceres* (Exeter, 1781); the Reverend
Robert Lucas, *Homer's Hymn to Ceres* (London, 1781); David
Ruhnken, *Homeri Hymnus in Cererem* (Leiden, 1782), first complete
edition.

17. Herbert Anton, *Der Raub der Proserpina: Literarische Traditionen
eines erotischen Sinnbildes und mythisches Symbol* (Heidelberg, 1967).
This discusses the theme in literature from Dante to Osip Mandelstam.

18. *The Complete Works of Algernon Charles Swinburne*, ed. Sir
Edmond Gosse and Thomas J. Wise, vol. 1 (London, 1925), 200–206,
299–302, 336–42.

19. Walter Pater, *Greek Studies* (London, 1895), 79–155, 'The Myth
of Demeter and Persephone'.

20. *The Poems of George Meredith*, ed. Phyllis B. Bartlett, vol. 1 (New Haven and London, 1978), 221–38, 415–19.

21. *The Poems of Tennyson*, ed. Christopher Ricks, vol. 3 (Longman, 2nd edn, 1987), 162–9.

22. *The Poems of Tennyson*, vol. 1, 620–22 (*Tithon*, written 1833), vol. 2, 605–12 (*Tithonus*, longer version, 1859–60).

23. *Poetical Works of Robert Bridges* (2nd edn, Oxford, 1953), 49–85, 'Demeter – A Mask (Written for the ladies at Somerville College and acted by them at the inauguration of their new building in 1904)'.

24. Some other nineteenth-century English works inspired by this myth are Barry Cornwall, 'The Rape of Proserpine' (in *Poetical Works*, Paris, 1829, 37); Mary Shelley's verse drama *Proserpine*, written in 1820 (*Proserpine and Midas*, ed. André H. Koszul, London, 1922); Dante Gabriel Rossetti, 'Proserpine' (in *Collected Works*, ed. William M. Rossetti, vol. 1, London, 1890, 371); Jean Ingelow, 'Persephone' (in *Poems*, vol. 1, London, 1880, 181 ff.); Walter Savage Landor, 'Hymn to Proserpine' (in *Poetical Works*, ed. Stephen Wheeler, vol. 2, Oxford, 1937, 371); Lawrence Binyon, *Persephone: The Newdigate Poem* (London, 1890); and Dora Greenwell, 'Demeter and Cora', reprinted in *Victorian Women Poets: An Anthology*, ed. Angela Leighton and Margaret Reynolds (Oxford, 1995), 287–9.

25. André Gide, *Théatre Complet*, vol. 4 (Neuchatel and Paris, 1947), 113–53; and André Gide, *Proserpine, Perséphone*, ed. Patrick Pollard (Lyon, 1977), 30.

26. Helen Watson-Williams, *André Gide and the Greek Myth* (Oxford, 1967), 108–9.

27. Simone Weil, *Intuitions pré-chrétiennes*, ed. Père Jean-Marie Perrin (Paris, new edn, 1985), 9–13.

28. Most recently, the Australian composer Carl Vine has used the Greek text of the hymns to Earth, Moon and Sun, together with the opening verses of the Babylonian Creation Epic *Enuma Elish*, in his Choral Symphony No. 6, composed in 1995–6 (London, 1997).

Further Reading

Allen, T. W., Halliday, W. R. and Sikes, E. E., *The Homeric Hymns* (Oxford, 1936). Edition with introduction and commentary.

Burkert, W., *Greek Religion: Archaic and Classical* (Oxford, 1985). Authoritative general study of this subject.

Clay, J. S., *The Politics of Olympus. Form and Meaning in the Major Homeric Hymns* (Princeton, 1989). Detailed and comprehensive study of the longer hymns and their portrayal of the Olympian gods.

Foley, H. P., *The Homeric Hymn to Demeter* (Princeton, 1994). Considers the poem as an example of women's literature.

Hornblower, S. and Spawforth, A. (eds), *The Oxford Classical Dictionary* (3rd edn, Oxford, 1996).

Janko, R., *Homer, Hesiod and the Hymns* (Cambridge, 1982). Major study of linguistic and other criteria for dating and provenance of the hymns, in relation to other early epic poetry.

March, J., *Dictionary of Classical Mythology* (London, 1998).

Miller, A. M., *From Delos to Delphi* (Leiden, 1986). An excellent analysis of the structure of the 'Hymn to Apollo' and the question of its unity.

Richardson, N. J., *The Homeric Hymn to Demeter* (Oxford, 1974). Edition with introduction and commentary. The introduction discusses the hymn's place in the early epic tradition, religious character, literary qualities and later influence in antiquity.

Sowa, C. A., *Traditional Themes and the Homeric Hymns*

(Chicago, 1984). Analyses themes which are common to the hymns and other early Greek and Near Eastern mythology.

Some other English translations (in addition to those mentioned in the Introduction and the Translator's Note):

Athanassakis, A., *The Homeric Hymns* (Baltimore, 1976).

Boer, C., *The Homeric Hymns* (Dallas, 1979).

Crudden, M., *The Homeric Hymns* (Oxford, 2001).

Edgar, J., *The Homeric Hymns* (Edinburgh, 1891).

Lang, A., *The Homeric Hymns* (London, 1899).

Lucas, F. L., *The Homeric Hymn to Aphrodite* (Golden Cockerel Press, 1948).

Sargent, T., *The Homeric Hymns* (New York, 1975).

Way, A. S., *The Homeric Hymns, with Hero and Leander* (London, 1934).

West, M. L., *The Homeric Hymns and Homeric Apocrypha: The Lives of Homer* (Cambridge, Mass., 2003).

Translator's Note

The Greek text is basically taken from the text in the Loeb Classical Library, *Hesiod, The Homeric Hymns and Homerica*, with an English translation by Hugh G. Evelyn-White (Harvard University Press and William Heinemann Ltd, Cambridge, Mass., and London, 1914), which in turn follows the text established by T. W. Allen, *Homeri Opera* Tomus V (Clarendon Press, Oxford, 1912). The exception to this is hymn II, to Demeter, which takes the text given by Nicholas Richardson in his *The Homeric Hymn to Demeter* (Clarendon Press, Oxford, 1974). Occasionally, there are alternative readings of individual lines, and these have been reached through discussion with Nicholas Richardson.

I have not kept to the dactylic hexameter of the hymns, and have been loosely guided by the nature of the goddesses and gods as to what form the hymn should take. I have translated *anthropos* as 'human being' or some 'human'-based derivative (instead of 'man'), but *aner* I have translated as 'man' in its exclusively masculine sense: for example, in the 'Hymn to Dionysos' (I). The recurring epithets, such as 'cloud-gathering Zeus' or 'white-armed Hera' are not translated exactly the same each time they occur, on the grounds that their sense may change slightly with different rhythms and different contexts of meaning. Generally, I have tried to keep the original Greek endings for proper names and place names wherever possible, and not to give the Latin form even though it is sometimes more familiar. (An exception is Phoebus Apollo.)

Line numbering, by fives, follows the numbering in the original Greek text, and may not always reflect five lines of the English translation.

The Homeric Hymns

I

HYMN TO DIONYSOS

Some say it was at Drakanon,
some on windy Ikaros,
some in Naxos,
                    divine child,
                                    bull-god.

Others say it was beside
the deep whirling waters
of the river Alpheios
that Semele gave birth to you,
pregnant from Zeus who loves thunder.

Others, lord, say you were born at Thebes.   5

I say they lie.

The father of men and gods gave birth to you
far from human beings,
hiding you from white-armed Hera.

There is a certain Nysa,
a mountain peak flowering with forests,
far off in Phoenicia,
near the streams of Egypt.

No one comes there with his ship,   10
none of the human beings with the power of
    speech.

For it has no harbour,
no place to anchor for the swaying ships,
but sheer cliff circles it, very high
on every side, and it grows
many lovely, desirable things.

. . .

'And they will set up many statues in the temples.
As these things are three,
so every three years forever
shall mortals sacrifice to you
perfect hecatombs at your festivals.'

The Son of Kronos spoke
and nodded with his dark brows.
And the heavenly hair of the lord
flowed down from the immortal head
and he made great Olympos tremble.
Wise Zeus had spoken and nodded his head.

Be gracious, you
                      women-maddening
                                      bull-god.

We, the poets,
beginning and ending, we sing of you.
Anyone who forgets you
cannot remember sacred song.

I greet you, Dionysos,
god who appears as a bull,
you and your mother Semele,
whom they call Thyone.

II

HYMN TO DEMETER

Demeter with her lovely hair,
revered goddess, I begin to sing of her
and her daughter with the slender ankles,
whom Aidoneus seized, and loud-thundering,
far-seeing Zeus gave her away.

Far off from Demeter,
with her golden sword and her glorious harvests,
the daughter was playing
with the deep-breasted daughters of Okeanos,   5
she was gathering flowers, roses and crocuses
and beautiful violets in a soft meadow.
There were irises and hyacinths and a narcissus
which Gaia grew as a snare
for the girl with eyes like buds
to please the God Who Receives So Many
– for Zeus had willed it –
and the flower shone wondrously.

Everyone who saw it was amazed,   10
deathless gods as well as human beings.
From its root there grew a hundred blooms
which had a scent so sweet that all
the wide heaven above and all the earth
and all the salt swelling of the sea
laughed aloud.

15   And the girl too wondered at it,
     she reached out both her hands to take
     the lovely toy, but the earth with wide paths
     gaped open in the plain of Nysa,
     and He Who Receives So Many, the lord,
     sprang upon her with his immortal horses,
     the son of Kronos with many names.

     He caught hold of her, protesting,
     and he took her away, weeping,
     in his chariot of gold.
20   Then she screamed in a shrill voice,
     calling for her father, Son of Kronos,
     the highest and best.
     But no one, neither the deathless gods
     nor human beings, no one heard her voice,
     not even the olive trees heavy with fruit.
     Only the tender-hearted daughter of Persaios from
         her cave,
25   Hekate in her shining headband,
     and the lord Helios, brilliant son of Hyperion,
     they heard her crying for her father, Son of Kronos.
     But he sat apart from the gods, aloof
     in his temple of many prayers,
     accepting fine offerings from mortals.
30   So, although she resisted,
     the Ruler of Many and Receiver of Many
     drove her away on his immortal horses,
     his own brother's child
     – for Zeus had contrived it –
     the son of Kronos with many names.

     Yet the goddess, as long as she could see
     the earth and the sparkling sky
     and the fast-flowing sea full of fishes
35   and the light of the sun,
     and as long as she still hoped
     to look upon her dear mother

and the race of gods who live for ever,
then that hope charmed her great heart
in spite of her grief.
And the peaks of the mountains
and the depths of the sea echoed
with her immortal voice
and her noble mother heard her.

A sharp pain seized her heart.   40
With her lovely hands she tore the veil
from her long ambrosial hair,
and casting a dark-blue cloak over her shoulders
she streaked out like a wild bird
across dry land and sea, searching.

But no one wanted to tell her the truth,
neither the gods nor human beings,   45
and not even one true messenger
of the birds of omen came to her.
For nine days queen Deo roamed over the earth
with flaming torches in both her hands,
and she never once tasted ambrosia
and the sweet drink of nectar,
nor sprinkled water on her skin,   50
so deep in grief was she.
But when the tenth luminous dawn appeared,
Hekate came to meet her, holding a torch in her
        hands
and offering her news. She spoke to her and said:

'Queen Demeter,
bringer of seasons, giver of splendid gifts,
who of the heavenly gods or mortals
has carried away Persephone   55
and brought sorrow to your dear heart?
For I heard her voice but I did not see
with my eyes who it was.
I'm telling you quickly and truly all I know.'

So Hekate spoke.

60   And the daughter of Rhea with her lovely hair
      answered her not a word
      but darted swiftly away with her,
      flaming torches in both her hands.
      So they reached Helios,
      he who watches gods and men,
      they stood in front of his horses
      and the sacred goddess asked him:

      'Helios, will you give me honour as a goddess
65   if ever I have warmed your heart and soul
      with word or deed? The girl I bore,
      that sweet young shoot, lovely to look upon,
      I heard her sobbing in the empty air
      as if she were being forced against her will,
      though with my eyes I saw nothing.
      But you with your rays,
      you look down from the luminous air
70   on all the earth and all the sea,
      tell me your infallible truth about my dear child,
      if you saw her anywhere, who was it
      far away from me who seized her violently
      against her will and was gone
      – was it a god or a mortal man?'

      So she spoke.
      And the son of Hyperion answered her:

75   'Queen Demeter,
      daughter of Rhea with her lovely hair,
      you shall know. For I respect you greatly
      and pity you in your sorrow
      for your daughter with the slender ankles.
      There is no other god to blame
      but Zeus who gathers the clouds.
      He gave her to Hades, his own brother,

to be called his fair wife,   80
and Hades carried her off on his horses
and led her down into the realm of dusk
and darkness, screaming loudly.
But, goddess, cease your mighty weeping.
You must not nurse this rage,
which is so vain, so insatiable.
He is not unworthy as a son-in-law among the gods,
Aidoneus, Ruler of Many,
your own brother and your own blood.   85
Also he received his share of honour
when in the beginning the threefold division was made,
and he became lord of those with whom he lives.'

Saying this, he called to his horses.
At his shout quickly they whirled
his swift chariot away like long-winged birds.

Pain sharper still and yet more savage   90
came into her heart. Outraged
with the Son of Kronos, shrouded in his dark clouds,
she withdrew from the company of gods
and from high Olympos, and she went
to the cities of mortals and their rich fields,
disguising her form for a long time.
And no one who saw her knew her,
no man or deep-breasted woman,   95
until she came to the house of wise Keleos,
the lord of fragrant Eleusis.

Sad at heart, she sank down
by the side of the road at the Maiden Well,
where the citizens came to draw water.
She sat in the shade, with the branches
of an olive tree growing overhead.   100
And she was like an old woman, born long ago,
cut off from child-bearing

and the gifts of Aphrodite, lover of garlands,
like the nurses of the children of kings who deal justice
or like the housekeepers in their echoing halls.

105   The daughters of Keleos Eleusinides
saw her as they came for the water,
which was easy to draw there in pitchers of bronze,
to carry it home to their dear father.
There were four of them in the flower of maidenhood,
like goddesses – Kallidike and Kleisidike
110   and lovely Demo and Kallithoe, the oldest of all.
They did not recognize her,
for it is hard for mortals to see the gods.
Standing beside her, they spoke to her winged words:

'Old mother,
where are you from? And who are your parents
who must have been born long ago?
Why have you gone so far away from the city,
and do not come near the houses?
115   There are some women in the shady halls
who are as old as you, and others younger,
and they would welcome you in what they say and do.'

So they spoke. And she,
the queen among goddesses, answered them and said:

'Dear children, whoever you are among women,
120   greetings. I will tell you my story.
For it is not wrong to tell the truth
in answer to your question.
Doso is my name, which my honoured mother gave me.
I have just now come from Crete
over the broad back of the sea,
and not by my own wish, for pirates brought me
125   with force and violence, against my will.
Then they landed with their swift ship at Thorikos,

and there the women stepped all together on to the
    shore,
and the men also, and they prepared a feast
by the stern of the ship.
But my heart wanted no delicious food,
and secretly I ran away across the dark country   130
and escaped my arrogant masters,
so they should not take me across the sea to sell me
when they did not buy me.
So in my wanderings I have come here,
and I do not know what land this is,
or who the people are.
But may all those who live on Olympos   135
grant you husbands and the birth of children
parents long for. So take pity on me, girls,
and tell me truly, please, dear children,
whose house I can go to, what man or woman's,
where I might work for them graciously,
the kind of work that suits a woman no longer
    young.   140
Gladly would I nurse a new-born child, cradling him
in my arms, and I could look after the house
and make up the master's bed in a corner
of his well-built room and teach the women their work.'

So said the goddess. And immediately Kallidike,   145
a girl still unmarried and the loveliest
of the daughters of Keleos, answered her:

'Mother, we who are human have to endure
what the gods give even though we suffer.
For they are much stronger than we are.
I shall advise you clearly, and tell you the names
of the men who have great power and honour here,   150
those who are the leaders of the people,
who defend the towers of the city
with their decisions and straight judgements.

There is Triptolemos, subtle in mind,
and Dioklos and Polyxeinos and irreproachable
        Eumolpos
155   and Dolichos, and our own brave father.
And the wives of all these men
take care of their homes.
There is not one of those women
– once she had seen your face –
who would scorn you and turn you away from their
        home,
but they would welcome you, for you look like a
        goddess.
160   But if you would like to, wait here,
and we will go to our father's house and tell all this
to our mother, deep-breasted Metaneira,
so that she might persuade you to come to our house
and not search for anyone else's.
She has an only son, born late to her,
who is being nursed in our well-built palace.
165   He was much longed for and welcome indeed.
If you were to take care of him
until he becomes a young man,
any woman who sees you would at once envy you,
so great a reward for his upbringing
would my mother give you.'

So she spoke, and the goddess nodded her head.
170   Then they filled their shining pitchers with water
and carried them away in delight, and swiftly
they reached their father's great house
and soon told their mother all they had seen and heard.
She urged them to run and invite her
to come for a limitless wage.

And just as in spring
deer and calves leap in the meadows
175   when they have eaten grass to their hearts' delight,
so the girls gathered up the folds

of their shimmering gowns and darted
down the hollow road, their long flowing hair
tossing about their shoulders like crocus flowers.

They found the glorious goddess near the road
where before they had left her,
and then they led her to their father's house.   180
She walked behind them, her dear heart grieving,
her head veiled, and the dark-blue cloak
swirled around the delicate feet of the goddess.

Soon they reached the house of Keleos,
whom the gods cherish, and they went through the
          portico   185
to where their lady mother sat beside a pillar
of the close-fitting roof, holding in her lap
her child, a new shoot. The girls ran to her.
But the goddess stepped on the threshold,
her head touched the roof,
and she filled the doorway with divine radiance.
Awe and reverence and pale terror seized the mother.   190
She yielded her couch to the goddess,
urging her to sit. But Demeter,
who brings the seasons, whose gifts are so brilliant,
did not wish to sit down on the shining couch,
but waited in silence, her beautiful eyes cast down,
until Iambe, who was sensitive and thoughtful,   195
set before her a strong stool, throwing over it
a silver fleece. Then the goddess sat down
and drew her veil over her face with her hands.
And for a long time she sat upon the stool
voiceless with grief, acknowledging no one
by word or deed, not smiling,
not tasting any food or drink,   200
she just sat there, wasting with longing
for her deep-breasted daughter,
until Iambe, so sensitive and thoughtful,
changed the mood of this sacred lady with jokes

and many jests and made her smile and laugh
and put an end to her sadness.

205 In later times also it was Iambe
who pleased the moods of the goddess.
Then Metaneira filled a cup with the honey-sweet wine
and gave it to her, but she refused.
It was not lawful, she said, for her to drink red wine.
She asked them to mix barley meal and water
with soft mint and give her that instead.

210 So Metaneira mixed the *kykeon*, as she was told,
and offered the cup to the goddess.
And the great queen Deo accepted it for the sake of the
        rite.

Then Metaneira in her lovely gown was the first to speak:

'Greetings, lady, for I believe you come from parents
who are not lowly but noble.
Dignity and grace show clearly in your eyes,

215 as they do with kings who administer justice.
But we who are human have to endure gifts from the
        gods
even though we suffer, for a yoke lies upon our necks.
But now that you have come here, all that is mine shall
        be yours.
Nurse this child for me, whom the gods gave me late in
        my life
when he was past hoping for, in answer to my many

220   prayers.
If you take care of him till he becomes a young man
any woman who sees you will at once envy you,
so great a reward for his upbringing will I give you.'

Then rich-crowned Demeter answered her:

225 'Greetings to you too, lady, may the gods be good to you.
I will gladly accept the child, as you ask me,
and nurture him for you, and I do not think

witchcraft or the Undercutter will harm him
through any evil design of his nurse.
For I know a charm more cutting than the
    Woodcutter
and I know a strong safeguard against harmful
    witchcraft.'   230

As she said this, she took the child
to her fragrant breast with her immortal hands.
And his mother was happy in her heart.
So in the palace the goddess nursed Demophoon,
the splendid son of the wise Keleos,
whose mother was the fair Metaneira.
And he grew up like a god, not eating food   235
nor suckling his mother's milk.
For Demeter anointed him with ambrosia
as though he were born from a god,
breathing on him sweetly as she held him to her
    breast.
But at night she buried him in the heart of the fire,
like a torch, without his dear parents knowing.   240
And it was a great wonder to them
how he grew far beyond his years,
and he was in appearance like a god.
And the goddess would have made him ageless,
    deathless,
if the lovely Metaneira, without thinking, had not
    looked out
one night from her fragrant chamber and spied.

She screamed, she beat both her thighs,   245
terrified for her child, blinded in her spirit,
and she cried out winged words, wailing:

'Demophoon, my son,
the stranger buries you deep in the fire
and makes me weep and gives me bitter pain.'

250 So she spoke, lamenting.
     And the divine goddess heard her.
     Lovely-crowned Demeter was enraged,
     she snatched the dear child out of the fire
     with her immortal hands – the child
     born in the palace when it was past hoping for –
     and she threw him away from her on to the ground,
     her heart seething with fury.
     Then she spoke directly to Metaneira in her lovely
255   gown:

     'How ignorant are human beings, how mindless they
          are,
     not to foresee the destiny that is coming towards them,
     not to know whether it is good or whether it is bad.
     In your senseless folly you have done wrong past cure.
     Let the oath of the gods, the implacable
     waters of Styx, be my witness.
260 I would have made your dear child deathless, ageless,
     all his days, I would have given him everlasting honour.
     But now it is impossible for him
     to escape the fate of death.
     Yet this undying honour shall always belong to him
     – that he lay on my lap and slept in my arms.
265 But in due season, as the years come round for him,
     the sons of Eleusis will wage war with each other
     and have terrible battles continually and forever.

     I am Demeter, the honoured one,
     who for mortals and immortals alike
     has been made the greatest blessing and source of joy.
270 But come, let all the people build for me a great temple
     and an altar beneath it, below the steep walls of the city
     above Kallichoron, upon the rising hill.
     And I myself will inaugurate my mysteries,
     so that from now on you may perform them in all purity
     and be reconciled to my heart.'

As the goddess said this, she changed her stature and
        form,   275
throwing away old age. And beauty breathed all
        around her
and a lovely fragrance drifted from her perfumed robes
and from the immortal skin of the goddess a brightness
shone far away from her and her golden hair streamed
        down
over her shoulders so that the solid house
was filled with light like lightning.   280
Then she left the palace.

At once Metaneira's knees gave way,
and for a long time she was speechless,
she did not even remember to pick up her only son
from the floor. But his sisters heard his pitiful crying
and they sprang down from the richly spread couches.   285
One of them took the child in her arms
and held him to her breast, and another
rekindled the fire, and another one ran with soft feet
to rouse their mother from the fragrant chamber.
They gathered round the child who was shaking all
        over,
and washed him and cuddled him, but his heart   290
was not comforted, for the nurses and maids
who were holding him now were worse than before.

All night long, quivering with fear,
they tried to appease the glorious goddess.
But as soon as dawn appeared they told powerful
        Keleos
exactly what had happened, just as the goddess
had commanded, Demeter with her lovely crown.   295
So he called to assembly his innumerable people,
and he ordered them to build for Demeter with the
        lovely hair
a sumptuous temple and an altar upon the rising hill.
They heard his voice and hurriedly obeyed him,

building it as he commanded.
300   And it grew as the goddess decreed.

Now when they were finished and done with their
          labour,
each man went back to his house.
But golden-haired Demeter sat there,
far away from all the blessed gods
she stayed there, wasting with longing
for her deep-breasted daughter.
305   And she made a most terrible and cruel year
for human beings on the deeply nourishing earth.
The earth did not send up seed,
for rich-crowned Demeter kept it hidden.
Many times the oxen dragged the curved plough
across the fields in vain, and many times
the white barley fell upon the earth fruitlessly.
310   So she would have destroyed utterly
the mortal race of human beings, starving them
to death, and deprived those who live on Olympos
of the glorious honour of gifts and sacrifices,
if Zeus had not noticed it and reflected upon it in his
          heart.

First he sent Iris on her wings of gold
315   to call Demeter with her lovely hair,
so beautiful to look upon. He spoke,
and she obeyed Zeus, Son of Kronos, in his dark clouds,
and she ran swiftly between heaven and earth.
She reached the city of fragrant Eleusis
and found Demeter in her temple in her dark-blue cloak.
320   She called her and spoke to her winged words:

'Demeter, father Zeus,
whose knowledge is endless,
calls on you to come back among the race of gods
who live for ever. So come, do not let
the word of Zeus I bring you go unfulfilled.'

So she spoke, imploring her.
But the heart of the goddess was unmoved.
So then the father sent out all the blessed gods   325
who are forever, one after the other.
They went, each in their turn, calling her
and offering her many beautiful gifts and honours,
whatever she would choose among the gods.
But no one could persuade her mind or purpose
for she was seething in her heart.   330
Unrelenting, she spurned their words.
She vowed that never again would she walk
upon fragrant Olympos, nor would she let
the fruits of the earth come up
until she saw her daughter's beautiful face
with her own eyes.

Now when loud-thundering, far-seeing Zeus
heard this, he sent to Erebos
the Slayer of Argos with his golden wand   335
to win over Hades with soft words
and to lead Persephone out of the murky darkness
into the light among the gods
so that her mother would see her
with her own eyes and let her anger go.
Hermes did not disobey, and immediately leaving   340
the heights of Olympos he plunged down
at high speed into the secret places of the earth.
And he found the lord Hades inside his house,
seated upon a couch with his modest wife,
who was most unwilling, longing for her mother.
But her mother was far away,
brooding on her terrible plan,   345
because of what the blessed gods had done.

The strong Slayer of Argos
stood next to the god and said:

'Dark-haired Hades, lord of the dead,
Father Zeus ordered me to bring back
noble Persephone out of Erebos
to be with the gods so that her mother
350   will see her with her own eyes
and stop her anger, her terrible wrath
against the gods. Now she is planning
a dreadful deed, to destroy the feeble race
of human beings sprung from the soil,
burying their seeds beneath the earth,
and destroying utterly the honours of the immortals.
For she has a terrible rage
and does not mingle with the gods,
355   but sits apart in her fragrant temple,
far away from them in the rocky city of Eleusis.'

So he spoke. And Aidoneus,
lord of those beneath the earth,
smiled grimly, and did not refuse
the commands of king Zeus.
Immediately he called
the wise Persephone:

360   'Go now, Persephone, to your mother
in her dark-blue cloak and go with a kind heart.
Do not despair so excessively,
for I shall not be an unworthy husband
among the deathless gods,
I who am brother to your father Zeus.
While you are here you will reign over all
365   that lives and moves and you will have
the greatest honours among the deathless gods.
There will be eternal punishment for those
who do wrong and do not ritually appease your spirit
by performing sacred rites and making due offerings.'

370   So he spoke. And wise Persephone
was filled with joy and quickly jumped up

in delight. But he, stealthily,
gave her to eat a seed of the pomegranate,
honey-sweet, furtively peering around him,
so she would not stay away for ever
with the venerable Demeter in her dark-blue cloak.

Aidoneus, Ruler of Many, harnessed   375
his immortal horses to his chariot of gold.
And she mounted the chariot
beside the strong Slayer of Argos
who took the reins and the whip in his own hands
and raced out of the palace.
The horses, unresisting, flew away.
Quickly they covered the vast distance.   380
Neither the sea nor the water of rivers
nor the valleys of grass nor the mountain peaks
stopped the force of the immortal horses
but they cut deep into the air above them as they went.
Hermes drove them to the place
where rich-crowned Demeter was waiting,
and reined them in before the fragrant temple.   385

And when Demeter saw them she leaped
as a maenad leaps down a mountain
of dark woods while Persephone,
from the other side, saw the beautiful eyes
of her mother and sprang down
from the chariot and horses
and ran to her and threw her arms
round her neck and embraced her.
Demeter held her dear child in her arms   390
when, suddenly, her heart suspected treachery
and she trembled terribly.
She stopped hugging her and at once asked her:

'My child, tell me, you did not,
did you, eat any food while you were below?
Speak out and hide nothing from me

so we both may know. If you did not,
395   then you are free from loathsome Hades
and you will live with me and your father,
Son of Kronos in his dark clouds,
and be honoured by all the immortal gods.
But if you did eat anything you will have to go back
        again
to the secret depths of the earth and live there
for a third part of the seasons of the year,
but for the other two parts
400   you will be with me and the other immortals.
But whenever in spring the earth blossoms
with sweet flowers of every kind, then you will rise
        again
from the realm of dusk and darkness
and be a source of great wonder for mortals and for
        gods.
But tell me how he seized you away into the gloomy
        darkness,
what guile did he use to deceive you,
that mighty Receiver of Many?'

405   Then the very beautiful Persephone faced her and said:

'Mother, I shall tell you the whole truth.
When Hermes, who brings luck, came to me
as the swift messenger of father Zeus
and the other children of Ouranos
to bring me back out of Erebos
so you could see me with your own eyes and stop
410   your anger, your terrible wrath against the gods,
I leapt up at once for joy,
but secretly he slipped into my mouth a seed
from a pomegranate, that honey-sweet food,
and forced me, made me taste it against my will.
Also I will tell you how he came and seized me
because of the shrewd scheming of my father,

Son of Kronos, and how he carried me down
into the secret depths of the earth, 415
I will tell you and reveal everything as you asked:

We were all playing in a lovely meadow,
Leukippe and Phaino and Electra and Ianthe,
also Melite and Iache with Rhodeia
and Kallirhoe and Melobosis and Tyche 420
and Okyrhoe, the beautiful flower,
and Chryseis, Ianeira, Akaste and Admete
and Rhodope and Plouto and lovely Kalypso
and Styx and Ourania and lovable Galaxaura,
with Pallas who starts fights
and Artemis who loves arrows,
we were playing and gathering 425
sweet flowers in our hands,
soft crocus mingled with irises
and hyacinths and rosebuds
and lilies – wondrous to see –
and a narcissus which the wide earth grew,
yellow as a crocus.
I picked it in delight, but the earth opened
beneath. And then the mighty lord, 430
He Who Receives So Many, sprang out
and carried me away beneath the earth
even though I resisted, in his chariot of gold.
Then I cried out with a shrill cry.
All this is true even though
it grieves me to tell you it.'

So then all day long, united in heart,
they greatly warmed each other 435
in soul and spirit, embracing continually,
and their hearts stopped grieving.
They gave and received joy from each other.
Then Hekate came towards them in her shining
    headband,

and many times she embraced the sacred daughter
        of Demeter,
and from that time the lady Hekate
440 was her follower and friend.

Then loud-thundering, all-seeing Zeus
sent a messenger to them
– Rhea with her lovely hair –
to bring Demeter in her dark-blue cloak
back to the tribes of gods,
and he promised to give her honours,
whatever she chose among the immortal gods,
445 confirming with a nod that her daughter would live
in the kingdom of dusk and darkness
for a third part of the circling year,
but for the other two parts she would live
with her mother and the other immortals.

So he spoke. And the goddess
did not disobey the message of Zeus.
Quickly she darted down the peaks of Olympos
450 and came to the plain of Rarion,
a land once life-giving and fertile with corn
but fruitful no longer, lying fallow
and leafless everywhere, the white barley
buried by Demeter's design,
she whose ankles are so beautiful.
But soon, with the coming of spring,
it would grow long ears of corn like waving hair,
455 and the rich furrows of soil would be heavy
with grain to be bound up in sheaves.
There the goddess first landed out of the barren air,
and the goddesses were glad to see each other,
and their hearts were filled with joy.
Then Rhea in her shining headband said to Demeter:

'Come, my child,   460
loud-thundering, far-seeing Zeus calls you
to come back to the tribes of gods,
and he has promised to give you honours,
whatever you wish among the immortal gods.
He consented with a nod that for a third part
of the circling year your daughter
shall go down to the gloomy darkness,
but for the other two parts she shall be   465
with you and the other immortals.
So he has said it would be, and he nodded his head.
But come, my child, obey him,
and do not be so excessively angry
with the Son of Kronos in his dark clouds.
Quickly, make the grain grow that gives the humans
    life.'

So she spoke. And rich-crowned Demeter   470
did not refuse. Immediately she let the crops
spring up from the rich fields
and the whole wide earth was laden with leaves and
    flowers.
Then she went to the kings who administer justice
– Triptolemos and Diokles who drives horses
and strong Eumolpos and Keleos, leader of the
    people –   475
and she revealed to them the celebration
of her awesome rites and taught them all her mysteries,
sacred mysteries which no one may transgress in any
    way
or inquire into or speak about,
for great awe of the gods stops the voice.
Blessed is the one of all the people on the earth   480
who has seen these mysteries.
But whoever is not initiated into the rites,
whoever has no part in them,

that person never shares the same fate when he dies
and goes down to the gloom and darkness below.

Now when the queen among goddesses
had taught them everything,
she and her daughter went to Olympos,
to the company of the other gods.
485   And there they live beside thunder-loving Zeus,
these sacred and venerable goddesses.
And very blessed is the one
of all the people on the earth whom they freely love.
Immediately they send Ploutos as a guest
to that one's great house,
he who gives abundance to mortals.
490   But come now, you who have your home
in the land of sweet Eleusis,
and Paros with the sea flowing round it,
and rocky Antron, you, queen,
you give us glorious gifts,
you bring the seasons,
sovereign Deo,
you and your daughter,
the surpassingly beautiful Persephone,
be gracious to me, and for my song
grant me a life my heart loves.
495   And now I shall remember you and another song too.

III

HYMN TO APOLLO

DELIAN APOLLO

I shall remember,
may I not forget,
Apollo the Archer.

The gods tremble at him
when he enters the house of Zeus,
they spring up when he comes near them,

they all spring up from their seats
when he stretches back his bright bow.
Only Leto waits beside Zeus who loves thunder.   5

She unstrings the bow, she closes the quiver,
taking it with her hands
off his strong shoulders,

she hangs the bow on a golden peg
against a pillar in his father's house.
Then she leads him to a seat.

His father gives him nectar in a golden cup,   10
he welcomes his dear son.
The other gods greet him and then sit down.

Queen Leto is full of joy
because the son born to her
is an archer and strong.

Be happy, blessed Leto,
you have given birth to glorious children,
15   the lord Apollo and Artemis who delights in arrows,

her in Ortygia, and him among the rocks of Delos,
leaning against the vast crag of the Kynthian hill,
close to a palm tree by the streams of Inopos.

How then shall I sing of you,
who are sung in every song?
20   For you, everywhere, Phoebus,

the fields of song are laid out,
on the mainland which rears our calves
and on the islands.

All the mountain peaks delight you,
the jutting headlands of rising hills,
rivers flowing out to sea,

capes leaning towards the sea,
harbours too,
all these delight you.

25   Shall I sing how first Leto gave birth to you
– the joy of mortals –
lying against Mount Kynthos

on that rocky island Delos, swirled around by sea,
while on both sides a black wave rolled over
to the land in shrill winds,

and how because of this, your origin,
you rule over all human beings?
The people of Crete and the city of Athens,   30

the island of Aigina and Euboea, famous for ships,
Aigai, Eiresiai and Peparethos by the sea,
Thracian Athos and the towering peaks of Pelion,

Thracian Samos and the shadowy mountains of Ida,
Skyros, Phokaia and the high hill of Autokane,   35
well-built Imbros and misty Lemnos,

holy Lesbos, the home of Makar, son of Aiolos,
and Chios, the brightest of all
the islands that lie in the sea,

craggy Mimas and the steep slopes of Korykos,
gleaming Klaros and the sheer peaks of Aisagee,   40
well-watered Samos and the precipitous heights of
    Mykale,

Miletos and Kos, the city of the Meropian people,
rugged Knidos and windswept Karpathos,
Naxos and Paros and rocky Rhenaia –

to all these places Leto came,   45
labouring to give birth to the far-shooting god,
to see if any of these lands

would be willing to make a home for her son.
But they all trembled, they were utterly terrified
and not one of them dared to accept Phoebus,

not even the richest of them,
until Leto, the queen, stepped on to Delos
and asked her, uttering winged words: 50

'Delos, would you be willing
to be the home of my son, Phoebus Apollo,
and to make him a sumptuous temple?

No other god will touch you,
or honour you,
and I do not think you will ever be

rich in cattle, rich in sheep,
you will never give good wine,
or grow many plants.

But if you have the temple of far-working Apollo,
then all the people will gather here,
bringing their hecatombs,

and the ineffable smell of sacrifice
will rise up for ever, and you will feed
your own people who live here

out of the hands of strangers,
for your own soil is barren.'
This is what she said.

And Delos was full of joy
and answered her and said:
'Leto, most glorious daughter of great Koios,

I would gladly receive your child,
the far-shooting lord. It is true
that people say terrible things about me,

while this way I should become very highly
          honoured.
But, Leto, there's a rumour I tremble at,
I won't hide it from you.

They say Apollo will be very presumptuous,
that he will dominate gods and mortals
all over the earth that gives us grain.

So I'm very afraid in my heart and soul   70
that as soon as he first sees the light of the sun
he will despise this island,

– since I am truly a rocky land –
and then he'll turn me over with his feet
and thrust me down into the depths of the sea,

and then the great waves of ocean
will wash over my head forever,   75
and he'll go away to another land,

one that pleases him, and build there
his temple and his shaded groves.
Then sea creatures with many feet

will make their lairs in me,
black seals, undisturbed, will make their
    homes in me,
because I am destitute of people.

But, goddess, if only you would dare
to swear a great oath?
That here, first, he will build   80

a very beautiful temple
to be an oracle for human beings
and only afterwards among all the other people,

because there's no doubt he'll be very famous.'
This is what Delos said.
And Leto swore the great oath of the gods:

'Now Earth be my witness
and vast Heaven above
85   and Styx with your water cascading down

(this is the strongest, the most terrible oath
the blessed gods can swear)
hear this:

Phoebus shall have his fragrant altar
and his sacred precinct here, forever,
and he shall honour you beyond all others.'

Now when Leto had sworn and ended her oath
90   Delos was filled with joy
at the birth of the Lord who shoots so far.

But Leto was pierced with the pain of labour,
for nine days, for nine nights,
she suffered unimaginably.

All the goddesses were there,
all those who most mattered,
Dione and Rhea and Ichnaean Themis

and Amphitrite who moans so loudly,
and the other immortal goddeses,
95   all except white-armed Hera.

She sat in the halls of cloud-gathering Zeus.
Only Eileithyia, the goddess
who helps women in labour, did not hear about it.

She was sitting on top of Olympos beneath golden
        clouds
– white-armed Hera contrived it –
100   she kept her away through envy

because lovely-haired Leto was destined to give birth
to a son who would be flawless and strong.
So the goddesses sent Iris out of the well-built island

to bring Eileithyia, and they promised her
a great necklace fastened together
with threads of gold, nine cubits long.

They told Iris to call her aside,   105
away from white-armed Hera, lest Hera, with her
        words,
might afterwards persuade her not to go.

When Iris – whose feet are as fast as the wind –
heard this, she started running
and she soon covered the whole distance.

And when she reached the home of the gods,
sheer Olympos, immediately she called Eileithyia   110
out of the hall to the door and spoke to her

winged words, telling her everything,
just as the goddesses who live on Olympos
had urged her to.

So she won over Eileithyia's heart,
and they went away, stepping softly
on their feet like shy wood doves.

Now as soon as Eileithyia, the goddess   115
who helps women in labour,
touched Delos, the moment of birth

seized Leto and she longed to deliver.
She threw her arms around the palm tree
and pressed her knees into the soft meadow.

Beneath her the earth smiled.
Then the child leapt out into the light
and all the goddesses screamed.

120   There, great Phoebus,
        the goddesses washed you with fresh water,
        purely and cleanly,

        and they wrapped you in a white cloth,
        which was finely spun and newly made,
        and around you they fastened a golden band.

        Now Apollo's mother did not suckle him,
        the god who carries the golden sword,
        but Themis poured for him nectar

125   and the lovely ambrosia with her divine hands.
        Leto was glad because she had given birth
        to a son who was an archer and strong.

        But, Phoebus, the moment you swallowed
        the heavenly food, the gold cords
        could no longer hold you, struggling,

        the bonds could not restrain you,
        for all the ends came loose.
130   Immediately, Phoebus Apollo

        addressed the immortal goddesses:
        'May the lyre and the curved bow be dear to me,
        and I shall reveal to mortals

        the infallible will of Zeus.'
        With these words, Phoebus,
        the long-haired, far-shooting god,

began walking over the wide paths of the earth.
All the goddesses were astonished.   135
And all of Delos flowered with gold,

like a mountain peak when the forest flowers,
when she saw the child of Zeus and Leto,
in joy because the god chose her

to be his home
over the islands and the mainland,
and loved her dearly in his heart.

And you, far-shooting Apollo,   140
lord of the silver bow,
at one time you went walking on rugged Kynthos,

at another time you wandered
among the islands and among mankind.
Many temples belong to you, many shaded groves,

and all the mountain peaks are dear to you,
all the sheer cliffs of high mountains,
all the rivers running to the sea.   145

But, Phoebus, it is Delos
that most delights your heart. There for your sake
the Ionians gather in their trailing robes

with their children and their revered wives.
There they delight you with boxing and dancing
and song, remembering you   150

whenever they hold their festivals.
Anyone who happened to meet them,
the Ionians, gathered there together,

would say they were immortal,
that they would never grow old.
For he would see the grace in all of them,

and would be glad at heart, watching
the men and the beautifully dressed women
155   with their swift ships and their great wealth.

And besides, there's this great wonder
whose fame will never die:
the girls of Delos,

servants of the lord who shoots so far,
first they sing to Apollo, then to Leto
and to Artemis who delights in arrows,

and then they sing a song recalling
160   the men and women who lived long ago,
and so they enchant the tribes of human beings.

They know how to imitate the sounds
and the chattering talk of all peoples.
Their song is so lovely,

so finely crafted,
that each person would think
he were speaking himself.

165   But come now, Apollo and Artemis, be gracious,
and all you girls, farewell.
Remember me in the time to come,

whenever someone on this earth
– a stranger who has suffered many things –
arrives here and asks you:

'Girls,
who is the sweetest man of all the singers   170
who comes here to you,

who is it most delights you?'
Answer him together, all of you,
with one voice:

'The blind man who lives in rocky Chios,
all his songs will be the best,
now and in the time to come.'

As for me, I shall carry your fame
wherever I wander over the earth
to the cities of human beings   175

settled in fine places.
And they will believe me
because it is true.

I shall never stop
singing hymns for Apollo,
god of the silver bow

who shoots so far,
child of Leto
with her beautiful hair.

O Lord, Lykia and enchanting Meonia
are yours, and Miletos,
lovely city of the sea,
but you reign yourself supremely over Delos,
washed all around with waves.

The glorious son of Leto
goes on his way to rocky Pytho,
playing his hollow lyre,
and wearing divine and fragrant clothes.
At the touch of his plectrum of gold
the lyre makes an enchanting sound.
Then, like a thought,
he goes from earth to Olympos,
to the house of Zeus,
to the gathering of the other gods.

And suddenly the gods think only
of the lyre, think only of song,
and at the same time and all together
the Muses sing, voice
to sweet voice answering,
they sing of the divine gifts of the gods
and of the sufferings of human beings
which the gods bring upon them,
how they live, mindless, helpless,
how they can't find a cure for death,
can't stop old age.

Then the lovely-haired Graces
and the kind-hearted Hours dance
with Harmonia and Hebe and Aphrodite,
daughter of Zeus, holding each other
by the wrist. And there's someone
dancing with them who is not ugly,

180

185

190

195

not puny, but very great in stature
and wonderful to look upon.
That is Artemis, delighting in her arrows,
the sister of Apollo.
There is Ares playing with them   200
and the Slayer of Argos
with his far-seeing eyes.
Phoebus Apollo plays his lyre,
striding amongst them
with high and beautiful steps,
and a radiance shines off him, flashing
from his feet and fine-spun gown.
Golden-haired Leto and wise Zeus
delight in their great hearts   205
as they look upon their dear son
playing with the immortal gods.

How then shall I sing of you
who are sung in every song?

Shall I sing of you as a lover, seeking love?
How you went courting the daughter of Azan
with god-like Ischys, son of Elatos   210
who has fine horses? Or with Phorbas,
son of Triops, or with Ereutheus
or with Leukippos and the wife of Leukippos,
you on foot and he with his horses,
though he was just as good as Triops?

Or shall I sing how in the beginning
you went all over the earth,
searching for a place to have your oracle   215
for human beings, Apollo, you who shoot so far?

First you went to Pieria, coming down
from Olympos and passing by sandy Lektos
and the Aenianes and going through the land
of the Perrhaebi. Soon you came to Iolkos

and set your feet on Kenaion in Euboea,
famous for its ships. You stood
220   on the Lelantine plain but in your heart
you did not want to build your temple
and your shaded groves there.
So you crossed the Euripos,
Apollo, shooting so far,
and climbed up the sacred green hill,
and quickly you went on to Mykalessos
and the meadows of Teumessos and then
225   you came to the home of Thebe,
covered over with forest.
Nobody lived there yet in sacred Thebe,
and there were no paths, no roads yet
around the wheat plains of Thebe, just forest.

So you went still further, far-shooting Apollo,
and you came to Onchestos, Poseidon's shining
230   grove.
It is there that the colt who is newly broken in,
wearied at pulling a fine chariot, draws breath
when the good driver leaps to the ground
from his chariot and goes on his way.
Then the horses, released now from their master,
rattle the empty chariot for a while.
235   But if they break the chariot in the wooded grove,
the people take care of the horses but the chariot
is tilted upwards and left where it is.
For this was the rite from the very beginning.
The drivers pray to the lord,
but the chariot falls to the lot of the god.

From there you went still further,
far-shooting Apollo, and then you reached
the beautiful streams of Kephissos, pouring
240   forth
its sweet-flowing water from Lilaea.

You crossed over it, you who work from afar,
and you passed Okalea with its many towers
and you came to the grasslands of Haliartos.

Then you went towards Telphousa.
It delighted you, that tranquil place,   245
it was right for building a temple and a wooded
    grove.
You came very close to her and said:

'Telphousa, I'm inclined to build here
a very beautiful temple
to be an oracle for human beings,
where they will always bring me perfect hecatombs,
whether they live in the rich Peloponnesos   250
or in Europe or in all the wave-washed islands,
coming to seek the oracle.
And I shall deliver to all of them infallible counsel,
prophesying in my rich temple.'

With these words Phoebus Apollo laid out the
    foundations
which were broad and very long from end to end.   255
When Telphousa saw this, she was outraged
in her heart, and she spoke to him, saying:

'Phoebus, lord, who works from afar,
I will give you a word of advice,
since you are inclined to build
a very beautiful temple here
to be an oracle for human beings
who will always bring you perfect hecatombs.   260
Yet I will speak out and you
mark my words in your heart.
The pounding of fast horses
and the noise of mules watering
at my sacred springs will always annoy you,

and people would rather gaze
265   at the finely-made chariots
and the fast-footed horses thundering past
than at your great temple
and the many treasures inside it.
But if I might persuade you
– for you, lord, are stronger and mightier
than I and your power is very great –
build at Krisa beneath the cleft of Parnassos.
270   No bright chariot will clash there,
and there will be no stamping
of fast-footed horses
around your beautifully built altar.
But the glorious tribes of human beings
will bring gifts to you as "the Healer",
and with delight in your heart
you will receive beautiful sacrifices
from the people who live around there.'

275   With these words she swayed his mind,
so that she alone, Telphousa,
might have glory on earth,
not he, the Far-Shooter.

Still further yet you went,
far-shooting Apollo,
until you came to the city
of those arrogant men, the Phlegyes,
who had no care for Zeus and lived on this earth
280   in a beautiful glade near the Kephisian lake.
Then you raced up a mountain ridge
and came to Krisa beneath the snows of
        Parnassos,
where the shoulder of the mountain turns
towards the west, with a rock
hanging over from above
and a hollow rugged glade running underneath.

There the lord Phoebus Apollo   285
decided to make his lovely temple,
so he said this:

'It is here that I'm inclined
to build a very beautiful temple
to be an oracle for human beings
where they will always bring me perfect
        hecatombs,
whether they live in the rich Peloponnesos   290
or in Europe or in all the wave-washed islands,
coming to seek the oracle.
And I shall deliver to all of them infallible counsel,
prophesying in my rich temple.'

When he had said this, Phoebus Apollo
laid out the foundations
which were broad and very long from end to end.   295
And upon them the sons of Erginos,
Trophonios and Agamedes,
whom the immortal gods love,
built the threshold of well-based stones
to be a theme of song forever.
And the numberless tribes of human beings
lived around the temple.

There was a spring nearby,   300
flowing beautifully,
and there the lord, son of Zeus,
killed the great fat she-dragon
with his mighty bow,
a wild monster
who practised many evils
on the people of the earth,
both on the people themselves
and on their sheep with slender feet.
For she was a calamity of blood.

305 Once she received from Hera,
     who sits on a golden throne,
     the dreaded cruel Typhaon,
     and she brought him up
     to be a bane to mortals.
     Hera gave birth to him once
     when she was angry with father Zeus,
     because the Son of Kronos had given birth himself
     to glorious Athena from his head.
     The lady Hera was instantly furious,
310 and she said to the immortal gods
     who were gathered together:

     'Hear me, all you gods and goddesses,
     how Zeus who gathers the clouds
     already begins to dishonour me
     after he has made me his true-hearted wife.
     Without me, he gave birth to bright-eyed Athena
315 who is pre-eminent among all the blessed gods.
     But my son Hephaistos, whom I gave birth to myself,
     was born a weakling among all the gods,
     with his shrivelled foot. I took him
     with my own hands and threw him out
     and he fell into the deep sea.
     But silver-footed Thetis rescued him,
     the daughter of Nereus,
320 and she took care of him with her sisters.
     Would she had done some other favour
     to the blessed gods!
     O cruel and crafty one,
     what else have you got in mind?
     How dare you give birth to bright-eyed Athena
     all on your own?
     Wouldn't I have given you a child
     – I who was at least called your wife
325 among the deathless gods who hold wide heaven?
     You watch out now that I don't plot
     some evil for you in return.

Yes, actually, I shall bring it about
that a son is born to me
who will be foremost among the deathless gods,
and it will not shame the sacred bond
of marriage between you and me.
So I will not come to your bed,
but I'll go and stay with the immortal gods,   330
far away from you.'

When she had spoken, she went away from the gods,
her heart very angry. Then immediately
she prayed, the lady Hera with her cow-eyes,
and she struck the earth
with her hand flat against it, saying:

'Hear me now, Gaia, and broad Ouranos high
    above,
and you Titan gods who live beneath the earth   335
around great Tartaros from whom men and gods
    come.
Listen to me now, all of you,
and give me a child apart from Zeus
and one not lesser than him in strength.
Rather, may he be as much stronger than Zeus,
who sees all things, as Zeus, for his part,
is stronger than Kronos.'

This she cried, lashing the earth with her thick
    hand.   340
Then Gaia who gives life was moved.
When Hera saw it she was glad in her heart,
for by this she believed
her prayer would be fulfilled.
And from that time on, for a whole year,
she never came to the bed of cunning Zeus,
she did not even sit on her richly carved chair,
as she had done before, offering him good counsel.   345
Instead she stayed in her temples

where many people come to pray,
and she delighted in their offerings,
the lady Hera with her cow-eyes.

Now when the months and days were fulfilled
350   and the seasons came round again
with the turning of the year,
then she gave birth to one who was not
like the gods, not like mortals
– the dreaded, the cruel, Typhaon –
a scourge for human beings.
Immediately the cow-eyed lady Hera
took him and gave him to her
– this she-dragon –
so bringing one evil to another.
And the she-dragon received him.
355   But he practised many evils
on the famous tribes of human beings.

Whoever went to meet the she-dragon
the day of death would carry him off,
until the lord Apollo, who works from afar,
let fly at her his strong arrow.
Then, heavily, she lay there,
racked with bitter pain,
gasping for breath
and rolling about on the ground.
360   An unspeakable scream came into being,
a more than mortal sound.
All over the wood she writhed incessantly,
now here, now there, and then she gave up
her spirit, breathing out blood.

Then Phoebus Apollo boasted over her:

'Now you rot right here
upon the soil that feeds mortals.
You at least shall live no more

to be a monstrous evil to mortals
who eat the fruit of the earth that feeds so many   365
and who will bring here perfect hecatombs.
Typhoeus will not save you from a painful death,
neither will the infamous Chimaira,
but black Gaia and flaming Hyperion
will rot you right here.'

Phoebus said this, gloating over her,   370
and darkness covered her eyes.
Then the sacred power of Helios
made her rot away there,
and this is why the place is called Pytho
and why the people give the lord the name of
        Pythian,
because it was in this place that the piercing power
of Helios made the monster rot away.

Then Phoebus Apollo understood in his mind   375
that the sweet-flowing spring had deceived him,
and he started out in a fury against Telphousa
and reached her fast. He stood
very close to her and said this:

'Telphousa, you were not destined, after all,
to pour forth your sweet-flowing water,
deceiving my mind and keeping this lovely place   380
all to yourself. The fame of this place
shall be mine also, not yours alone.'
The lord Apollo who works from afar
said this and pushed a cliff down upon her
with showers of rocks and covered over her streams,
and he made himself an altar in a wooded grove
very close to the sweet-flowing spring.   385
In that place everyone prays to the lord,
calling him Telphousian, because he disfigured
the streams of sacred Telphousa.

Then Phoebus Apollo wondered in his heart
what kind of people he should bring
to celebrate his rites
390   and to be his priests in rocky Pytho.
And while he was musing on these things
he noticed there was a swift ship
on the wine-dark sea. There were many men in it,
and good men too, Cretans from Knossos,
the city of Minos, those who make sacrifices
to the lord and announce the decrees
395   of Phoebus Apollo with his golden sword,
whatever he speaks in answer from his laurel tree
beneath the hollows of Parnassos.

They were sailing in their black ship to sandy Pylos
and to the people of Pylos for trade and profit.
But Phoebus Apollo met them.
400   In the open sea, in the body of a dolphin,
he sprang upon their swift ship and lay there,
a huge and frightening monster.
Whoever among them had the heart to notice him,
the monster would shake him to and fro,
making the ship's timbers quiver.
They sat in silence in their ship, terrified.
405   They did not loose the sheets in the hollow black ship,
they did not lower the sail of the dark-prowed ship,
but as in the beginning they had set the course
with their oxhide ropes so they went sailing on.
And the rapid south wind drove on
the swift ship from behind.
First they passed by Maleia
410   and then along the Lakonian coast
until they came to that city Tainaron,
garlanded by sea, the country of Helios
who fills the hearts of mortals with joy.
Here the sheep of the lord Helios
with their thick fleece are always grazing,
they live in a land of delight.

The men wanted to land the ship there
and go ashore and think about this great wonder,   415
and see with their own eyes whether the monster
would stay on the deck of their hollow ship
or leap back into the swelling sea,
teeming with fishes. But the well-built ship
would not obey the helm, it kept on going,
all along the rich coast of Peloponnesos.
And the lord, far-working Apollo,   420
guided it easily with his breath.
So sailing on its course the ship reached Arene
and lovely Argyphea and Thryon, the ford of Alpheios,
and the well-placed Aipy and sandy Pylos
and the people born in Pylos.
It went on, past Krounoi and Chalkis and Dyme   425
and shining Elis where the Epeians rule.
While it was heading for Pherai,
delighting in the breeze from Zeus,
the steep mountain of Ithaka
appeared to them beneath the clouds,
and then Doulichion and Same and wooded
      Zakynthos.
But when they had passed along the whole
of the Peloponnesos, and when the boundless gulf   430
of Krisa came into view, which closes off
entirely the rich Peloponnesos,
then a great clear west wind came up
by the order of Zeus, blowing furiously
out of heaven, so that as soon as possible
the ship might end its journey
over the salt water of the sea.   435
So then they started sailing back
towards dawn and the sun.
And the lord Apollo, son of Zeus, led them.
They reached Krisa, the land of vines,
visible from afar, and so they put into harbour.
There the sea-going ship grounded on the sands.

440 Then the lord, the far-working Apollo,
leapt from the ship like a star at midday.
Flashes of fire flew off him all over
and a blaze of light reached to heaven.
He entered his shrine through the precious tripods
and he made a flame flare up, revealing
his gleaming arrows, and their bright light
filled the whole of Krisa.
445 The wives and daughters of Krisa
in their beautiful clothes
cried out at this radiance of Phoebus,
for he put great fear into each one of them.
Then, like a thought,
he sprang out again and flew back
to the ship in the shape of a man
who is lithe and strong – the flower
of youth – and his long hair
450 covered his broad shoulders.
He spoke clearly to the men,
uttering winged words:

'Strangers, who are you?
Where do you come from,
sailing along the wet paths of the sea?
Are you merchants or do you wander recklessly
over the waves like pirates
455 who roam around risking their lives
and bringing evil to strangers?
Why do you sit about like this being miserable,
why don't you go ashore
or put away the gear of your black ship?
For that is the custom of men
who work for their bread,
whenever they come in from the sea
to land in their black ships,
460 wearied with labour.
At once a longing for sweet food
catches hold of them about the heart.'

He said this and put courage in their hearts.
And the leader of the Cretans answered him and said:

'Stranger – though you are not like
mortal men, neither in size nor shape,
but are like the immortal gods –   465
greetings and good health to you,
may the gods give you good fortune.
Now tell me the truth so I may truly know.
What country is this? What land?
And what people live here?
For we had somewhere else in mind
when we went sailing over the great deep sea
to Pylos from Crete, the land we claim   470
as the place of our birth.
But now we have come here
with our ship to this place, not willing it at all,
and we long to go home
by another way, on other paths.
But one of the immortal gods
has brought us here against our will.'

Then far-working Apollo answered them and said:

'Strangers, you who once lived   475
around thick-wooded Knossos,
you shall now return no more,
not one of you to the city he loves
and his beautiful home and his dear wife.
Here, instead, you shall keep my rich temple
which will be honoured by many people.
For I am the son of Zeus.   480
I declare I am Apollo.
I led you here over the great deeps of the sea,
not meaning you any harm,
but so you would take care of my rich temple
which will be greatly honoured by all people.
You shall know the will of the immortal gods

and by their consent you shall always be
485   honoured,
every day and forever.
But come, quickly, do as I say.
First, loose the oxhide lines and lower the sails
and then haul the swift ship up on to the land.
Take the gear and your possessions
out of the well-balanced ship,
490   and make an altar on the sea shore.
Light a fire and sacrifice
white barley grains and then pray,
standing around the altar side by side.
And since at first in the misty sea
I sprang upon your swift ship as a dolphin,
495   pray to me as Delphinios.
And the altar also shall be Delphinios,
overlooking all things, forever.
Then have your meal beside your swift black ship
and pour an offering to the blessed gods
who live on Olympos.
But when you have satisfied your desire
for honey-sweet food, come with me,
500   singing the Paean in praise of the Healer,
until you come to the place
where you will keep my rich temple.'

He said this and they heard him closely
and obeyed him. First they loosened the lines
and let down the sail and lowered the mast
by the forestays into the mast-hold.
Then they themselves landed on the shore of the
505   sea.
They hauled the swift ship from the water
onto the land, high up on the sands,
and they stretched long beams beneath it.
Then they made an altar on the beach by the sea.
They lit a fire and sacrificed
white barley grains and prayed,

standing side by side around the altar,   510
as he had commanded.
Then they took their meal
beside the swift black ship
and poured an offering
to the blessed gods who live on Olympos.
And when they had satisfied
their desire for food and drink
they started to move.
And the Lord Apollo, son of Zeus,
led them, striding
with high and beautiful steps,   515
holding a lyre in his hands
and playing it beautifully.
So the Cretans followed him to Pytho,
stamping the earth in the dance
and chanting the Paean
like the paean-singers of Crete,
those in whose hearts the divine Muse
has put sweet-voiced song.
Tirelessly on foot they climbed   520
up the ridge and suddenly came
to Parnassos and the lovely place
where they were destined to make their home,
honoured by many people.
There he led them and showed them
his inner shrine and his rich temple.

But their spirit was roused in their dear hearts,   525
and the leader of the Cretans confronted him
      and asked him:

'Lord, since you have brought us here,
far away from our loved ones and our native land
– so it must have seemed good to your heart –
how are we now to live?
We beg you to consider this.
This place is not very pleasant,

either for bearing vines
or for rich pasture,
so as to let us live here well
530   and serve the people at the same time.'

Then Apollo, the son of Zeus, smiled at them
        and said:

'Foolish mortals, poor wretches are you
that you wish in your hearts
for cares and hard work and privation.
I'm going to give you a word of relief
and set this in your minds.
535   Let each one of you
with a knife in your hand
slaughter sheep forever
and there will still remain
an endless store,
everything, in fact, that
the glorious tribes of human beings
bring here for me.
So watch over my temple
and welcome the tribes of humanity
who gather here and above all
make known to them my will.
And keep justice in your hearts.
540   But if, in word or deed,
there is any vanity or arrogance
– for this is the custom of human beings –
then other men will be your masters,
and they will subdue you by force forever.
All has been told to you.
Guard it in your hearts.'

545   And so farewell, son of Zeus and Leto.
And now I shall remember you and another
        song too.

IV

HYMN TO HERMES

Sing, Muse, of Hermes, son of Zeus and Maia,
lord of Kyllene and Arcadia, the land of sheep,
messenger of the gods who brings luck,
born to Maia, the nymph with the beautiful hair,
the shy goddess who lay in love with Zeus.
She shunned the crowd of the blessed gods,   5
she lived in a shadowy cave, and there
in the depths of night the Son of Kronos
made love to the nymph with the beautiful hair
while sweet sleep held the white arms of Hera,
eluding the gaze of immortal gods and human beings.

Now when the mind of great Zeus was fulfilled   10
and the tenth moon was already fixed in the sky,
she brought forth into the light a child
and glorious deeds were accomplished.

She gave birth to a son who was versatile
and full of tricks, a thief,
a cattle-rustler, a bringer of dreams,
a spy by night, a watcher at the gate,   15
one who was destined to bring wonderful things
to light among the immortal gods.

Born at dawn, he played the lyre in the afternoon
and he stole the cattle of Apollo the Archer
in the evening – all on the fourth day of the month,
the day he was born from the lady Maia.

20   Now once he had leapt out
        from the immortal womb of his mother,
        he did not lie still for long
        in his sacred cradle but jumped up
        to look for Apollo's cattle, climbing over
        the threshold of the cave with the high roof.
        There he discovered the tortoise
        and won for himself infinite delight,
25   for Hermes was the first
        to make the tortoise a singer.

        It met him casually by the gates of the courtyard
        where it was eating the lush grass in front of the house,
        moving along on its awkward feet.
        The son of Zeus who brings luck looked at it
        and laughed, and said at once:

30   'Already an omen
             of great luck for me,
             I won't turn it down!
             Hello lovely creature,
             beating time to the dance,
             friend of the feasts,
             how exciting to meet you.
             Where did you get
             that beautiful toy from,
             that gleaming shell
             you wrap yourself up in,
             you, a tortoise,
             living in the mountains?
             I'm going to pick you up
             and take you home.
             You shall help me
35   and I won't shame you
             but you'll have to help me first.
             It's better to be at home
             when there's danger outside.
             Alive, you'd be a charm

> against vile witchcraft,
> but dead, you'll make
> such sweet song.'

As he said this, he lifted up the tortoise
in both his hands and ran back into the house,   40
carrying his lovely toy. Then, turning it over,
he scooped out the marrow with a knife of grey iron
from the tortoise who lived in the mountains.

Just as when a quick thought darts through the heart
of a man when cares crowd in on him
and toss him about or when bright glances spin   45
off the eyes – just like that –
glorious Hermes devised word and deed together.

He measured and cut stalks of reed
and fixed them in, he pierced through the back,
through the shell of the tortoise.
Inspired, he stretched oxhide over the shell,
put in the horns and fitted the crosspiece
over the two of them and stretched out   50
seven harmonious strings of sheep-gut.

When he had finished he took the lovely toy
and with a plectrum struck each string in tune,
and at the touch of his hand it resounded awesomely.
The god then, improvising, trying his skill, sang out   55
sweet snatches of song, just as at festivals
boys in the prime of youth mock and taunt each other.

He sang of Zeus, Son of Kronos,
and Maia in her beautiful sandals,
how they once used to talk in the friendship of love,
and he announced his origin, his own glorious name.
He celebrated also the handmaids of the nymph   60
and her shining home and the tripods about the house
and the abundant cauldrons.

But while he was singing of all this,
he was longing in his heart for other things.
So he picked up the hollow lyre
and laid it in his sacred cradle,
65 then he bounded out of the sweet-smelling room
to look around – he was hungry for meat –
musing in his heart some cunning trick,
the sort of thing thieves get up to
in the dark time of the night.

Helios was sinking beneath the earth into Ocean
with his horses and chariot when Hermes
70 came running to the shadowy mountains of Pieria,
where the sacred cattle of the blessed gods
had their stables and grazed on lovely untouched
           meadows.

Then the son of Maia,
the sharp-eyed Slayer of Argos,
cut off from the herd fifty cows
who were bellowing loudly.
75 He drove them across a sandy place the wrong way,
turning their tracks around.
He did not forget the art of trickery
when he reversed their hooves,
making the front hooves backward
and the back hooves forward
while he himself walked backwards.

Then, on the sand by the sea,
80 he wove sandals of wickerwork
– they were marvellous creations,
unthinkable, unimaginable –
tamarisk twisted round twigs of myrtle.
Then he fastened together armfuls
of fresh and budding wood and tied them
securely, with all their leaves,
as light sandals under his feet.

The glorious Slayer of Argos
gathered this brushwood in Pieria   85
as he was preparing for his journey,
like someone working it out for himself,
in a hurry with a long way to go.

An old man who was working
in his flowering vineyard
saw him rushing towards the plain
through the meadowland of Onchestos.
The son of glorious Maia
was the first to speak:

    'Old man, digging your plants   90
    with hunched shoulders,
    you're going to have
    a whole lot of wine
    when all these bear fruit
    just as long as you obey me
    and remember carefully that
    you didn't see what you just saw
    and you didn't hear what you just heard,
    so you keep quiet
    since there's no harm done
    to anything of yours.'

He said this and he hurried along
the strong cattle altogether.
Through many shadowy mountains   95
and echoing ravines and flowering plains
the glorious Hermes drove them on.

Divine night, his dusky helper,
was nearly over and dawn was soon coming,
calling the people to work.
Shining Selene, daughter of the lord Pallas,
son of Megamedes, had just ascended   100
to a new look-out place

when the brave son of Zeus
drove down to the river Alpheios
the wide-browed cattle of Phoebus Apollo.
Tirelessly they came to the stable
with the high roof and to the watering troughs
set down in front of a splendid meadow.

105   When he had fed the cattle well on the good pasture,
all of them bellowing loudly,
he herded them together and drove them
into the stable, still munching clover
and marsh plants sprinkled with dew.

Then he gathered wood into a pile
and tried to grasp the art of fire.
He took a branch of shining laurel,
gripped in the palm of his hand,
and trimmed it with a knife.

110   And hot smoke breathed upwards.
So Hermes was the first to invent fire
and firesticks for making it.
He took a large number of dry sticks
and piled them thickly in a hollow
dug out of the earth, and a flame glowed
and threw out a great blast
of blazing fire into the distance.

115   Now while the strength of glorious Hephaistos
was kindling the fire,
Hermes dragged out beside the fire
two bellowing cows with twisted horns
– he was filled with great power –
and threw them both panting
onto the earth on their backs.
Then he rolled them on their sides
and, forcing back their heads,
pierced through their marrows.

120   Now he moved from task to task,
cutting up the rich fatty meat.

He fixed it on spits of wood
and roasted the flesh and the chine
– the piece of honour –
and the entrails full of black blood.
These things were left lying in their place.
Then he stretched out their skins over a jagged rock
and even now, after so many years,   125
they are still there, a long long time
after these events, and will be without end.

Then Hermes with a happy heart
drew the rich meats on to a smooth flat stone
and divided them into twelve portions,
sharing them out by lot,
conferring upon each its due measure of honour.
But then glorious Hermes himself   130
longed for the sacrificial meat
– the delicious smell distressed him –
immortal though he was.
But his noble heart was not swayed
and no flesh passed down his sacred throat,
even though he yearned for it very deeply.
Instead he put away the fat and the abundant meat   135
in the high-roofed stable
and suddenly lifted them high up in the air
in remembrance of his youthful theft.
Then he gathered up wood for burning
and with the blast of fire he consumed them utterly,
with all their hoofs and all their thickly curled heads.

Now when the god had completed everything
that was due, he threw his sandals
into the deep whirling waters of Alpheios.
He quenched the embers, scattering   140
the black ash like sand all night long
while the beautiful light of Selene shone down.
At dawn he went straight back again
to the shining peaks of Kyllene

and no one crossed his path on his long journey,
neither the blessed gods nor human beings
145   – not even a dog barked.

Hermes, son of Zeus, who brings luck,
slid in sideways through the keyhole
and passed into the hall like a breeze
in autumn, like a mist.
He slipped straight through the cave
to the rich shrine, moving softly on his feet,
making no sound as one might upon the ground.
150   Then glorious Hermes climbed quickly
back inside his cradle and wrapped
his swaddling clothes around his shoulders,
and lay there like a helpless baby,
playing with the cloth around his knees
and covering his sweet lyre with his left hand.
But the god did not escape the eye
of his goddess mother who said to him:

155   'What are you up to, you rascal?
Where have you been,
coming home at this time of night,
clothed in your own impudence!
Now I'm quite sure you'll soon be bound
with unbreakable cords around your ribs
by the hand of that son of Leto
and then be thrown out of doors,
or you'll live a robber's life
up and down the valleys.
160   Away with you! Your father made you
to be a great nuisance to mortals
and to the deathless gods.'

Then Hermes answered her with cunning words:

'Mother, why do you try to
scare me like this

as if I were an infant child
who didn't know anything
and had no harm at all
in his heart,
a frightened baby in fact
who's afraid   165
of his mother's scolding?
No! I'm going to discover an art
– the best there is –
and so I'll be able to
feed myself and you forever.
We're not going to stay here
as you insist,
the only two
among the immortal gods
without any gifts
or any prayers.
It's much better   170
to spend every day
talking with the gods
and be rich and wealthy
and loaded with cornfields
than to sit here at home
in a gloomy cave.
As for honour,
I also will claim the rites
Apollo has.
And if my father won't
give them to me then I'll try
– and I can –
to be the prince of thieves.   175
And if the son of glorious Leto
comes after me
something else, even worse,
will happen to him.
For I'll go to Pytho
and break into his great house
and I'll carry off heaps

       of his beautiful tripods
       and cauldrons and gold
180   and piles of his gleaming iron
       and lots of clothing,
       and you shall see it all
       if you want to.'

With words such as these they spoke to each other,
the son of Zeus who holds the aegis and the lady Maia.

Now early-born Dawn was rising from the deep-flowing
            waters
185 of Ocean, bringing light to mortals, when Apollo
went on his way and came to Onchestos, the lovely
            grove
sacred to the loud-roaring god who holds up Earth.
There he found the old man working in the plot
of his vineyard by the side of the road.
The Son of glorious Leto was the first to speak:

190   'Old Man, bramble-picker from grassy Onchestos,
       I have come here from Pieria
       to look for my cattle,
       all of them cows
       and all with curving horns,
       they're from my herd.
       The bull was grazing alone,
       apart from the others, the black one.
       Four dogs with flashing eyes
       followed the cows,
195   all of one mind like people.
       They were left behind,
       the dogs and the bull,
       which is strange.
       And the sun was just sinking
       when the cows left the soft meadow,
       straying away from the sweet pasture.
       Tell me this, old man, born long ago:

have you seen a man driving my cows   200
along this road?'

Then the old man answered him with these words:

'My friend, it's hard to tell
all the things the eyes see.
For many travellers come along this road
– some intent on very bad things
others on very good things –   205
going up and down.
It's hard to know each one.
Still, I was here all day long
till the sun went down,
digging away in my plot of vines.
And I thought I saw a child,
but really, my good friend,
I don't know for sure,
and this child, whoever he was,
I think he was following some cattle
with beautiful horns,
he was only a baby,
he held a staff   210
and he kept walking from side to side.
He drove them along backwards
with their heads facing him.'

The old man spoke. The god listened to his words
and went more quickly on his way.
He saw a bird of omen with long wings
and instantly knew that the thief
had been born a child of Zeus, Son of Kronos.
The lord Apollo, son of Zeus, rushed eagerly on   215
to holy Pylos, searching for his cows
with their rolling walk, and covering
his broad shoulders with a purple cloud.
Then the Archer saw the tracks
and he spoke these words:

'Oh really!
What is this fantastic thing
I am seeing with my own eyes!
220   These are indeed the tracks
of my straight-horned cows,
but they are turned backwards
towards the flowering meadow.
Yet these others are not the footprints
of a man or a woman
or grey wolves or bears or lions.
Nor do I believe they are the tracks
of a centaur with a shaggy neck
225   – whatever it is that takes
such monstrous strides
on such fast-moving feet.
They are dreadful
on this side of the road,
but even more dreadful
on the other.'

He said this, the Lord Apollo, son of Zeus,
and rushed along and came to the mountain of Kyllene,
which is covered in forest, and the deep-shadowed
230   cave in the rock where the divine nymph
gave birth to the child of Zeus, Son of Kronos.
A lovely fragrance spread over the holy mountain,
flocks of sheep with slender feet grazed on the grass.
Then Apollo the Archer himself stepped swiftly
over the stone threshold into the dusky cave.

Now when the son of Zeus and Maia saw the Archer
         Apollo
235   in a rage about his cattle he sank down deeper
into his fragrant swaddling clothes.
Just as wood ash covers over the glowing embers
of tree stumps, so Hermes also curled himself up
when he saw the one who works from afar.
240   He squeezed his head and his hands and his feet

altogether in a small space, looking like a baby
just after his bath, inviting sweet sleep,
though actually he was wide awake
and holding on to his lyre under his armpit.
But the son of Zeus and Leto knew,
he did not fail to recognize
the beautiful mountain nymph and her dear son,
the little child wrapped up in crafty wiles.   245
He looked intently into all the recesses
of the great cave, then he took
a shining key and opened three chests
full of nectar and lovely ambrosia.
Much gold and silver lay inside them
and many of the nymph's dresses,   250
some dark-red, some silvery-white,
the kind of things that are kept
in the sacred houses of the gods.
Now when the son of Zeus and Leto had searched
the recesses of the great cave,
he said this to glorious Hermes:

     'You, child,
     lying in your cradle,
     just you hurry up and tell me
     where my cows are
     or you and I are going to   255
     fall out fast
     and there won't be any rules either.
     I'm going to take you
     and hurl you right down
     into black Tartaros
     into a dire and desolate darkness.
     And neither your mother
     nor your father
     will ever bring you back
     to the light of day
     but you'll wander under the earth
     and be the leader of the little people.'

Then Hermes answered him with
260   cunning words:

        'Son of Leto,
        why do you say
        all these horrid things?
        Have you come here
        to look for cows
        who live in meadows?
        I haven't seen them,
        I haven't heard them,
        I haven't even heard
        anyone talking about them.
        I can't tell you about them
        or win a reward for telling.
265   I'm not at all
        like a cattle driver,
        a strong man,
        that's no work for me.
        I care about other things.
        I care about sleep
        and my mother's milk
        and having wraps
        around my shoulders
        and warm baths.
        Let's hope no one hears
        what this quarrel is about!
270   It would be really amazing
        for the immortal gods
        to hear that a new-born child
        went right through the doorway
        with a herd of cows from the fields.
        You're talking nonsense!
        I was born yesterday,
        my feet are soft
        and the ground beneath is rough.
        But if you like,
        I'll swear a great oath

on my father's head:
I declare that I myself   275
am not guilty
nor did I see anyone else
stealing your cows,
whatever cows are
– I've only heard about them.'

While he said this, his eyes twinkled
                continuously
and he wriggled his eyebrows up and down,
glancing this way and that,
and he whistled too for a long time   280
like someone listening to an idle tale.
Far-working Apollo laughed softly
and said this to him:

'You rogue,
you trickster,
you crafty-minded cheat,
the way you talk
I can well believe
you broke into a good many
well-built houses last night
and left more than one man
with only the floor
to sit down upon,
packing up his home   285
without a sound.
You'll torment many shepherds
living in the forests
in mountain glades,
whenever you're craving for meat
and come across herds of cattle
and thick-fleeced sheep.
But come on now,
unless you want to sleep
your last and deepest sleep,

get out of your cradle,   290
companion of black night!
From now on you'll have
this honour among the immortal gods:
You will be called
the Prince of Thieves
for all time.'

With these words Phoebus Apollo picked up the child
and carried him off. But at that moment
the powerful Slayer of Argos conceived a plan
and as Apollo lifted him up in his hands
295   he let off an omen, an insolent servant
of the belly – a presumptuous messenger –
and immediately after this he sneezed.
Apollo heard it and threw glorious Hermes
out of his hands on to the ground.
Then he sat down in front of him
and even though he was impatient to leave
300   he spoke these words to Hermes, mocking him:

'Don't you worry,
little baby
in your swaddling clothes,
son of Zeus and Maia.
I shall find my strong cows soon
and by these very omens too.
And it's you
who'll lead the way there.'

He said this, and Kyllenian Hermes jumped up quickly
305   in a hurry to go. With both hands he rubbed his ears,
his blanket wrapped around his shoulders,
and then he said:

'Where are you taking me to,
Far-Worker,
most violent of all the gods?

Is it because of your cows
that you're so angry
and persecute me?
Oh dear! I wish
the whole race of cows
would just die!
It wasn't I
who stole your cows,
nor did I see
anyone else stealing them,
whatever cows are   310
– I've only heard about them.
Before Zeus, Son of Kronos,
give and take what is just.'

So they disputed each point exactly,
Hermes the shepherd and the glorious son of Leto,
their hearts divided – one of them speaking the truth   315
and not unjustly seizing glorious Hermes
for the sake of his cows, but the other, the Kyllenian,
trying with his tricks and winning words
to deceive the Lord of the Silver Bow.
But though he was very ingenious
he found the other was just as inventive,   320
so he walked quickly ahead across the sand
while the son of Zeus and Leto walked behind.

Soon they came, these very beautiful children of Zeus,
to the top of fragrant Olympos
to their father, the Son of Kronos.
There for both of them were the scales of justice set.
There was an assembly on snowy Olympos,   325
the imperishable immortals were gathering
as Dawn appeared on her golden throne.
Hermes and Apollo of the Silver Bow
stood before the knees of Zeus.
High-thundering Zeus questioned his brilliant son,
        and said:

330   'Phoebus, where have you come from,
          driving this sweet little prisoner,
          this new-born baby
          who has the look of a herald?
          This is a serious business
          to come before the council of the gods.'

     Then the lord, far-working Apollo, answered him:

          'O Father,
          you're about to hear
          no trifling tale
335   and you taunt me for being
          the only one who loves booty.
          This child,
          this absolute thief,
          I found in the mountains of Kyllene,
          at the end of a long journey
          through many lands
          – so full of mockery
          I've never seen anyone like him,
          not among the gods nor among those men
          who cheat people on the earth.
340   He stole my cows from their meadow,
          he drove them off in the evening
          along the shore of the loud-roaring sea
          and he headed straight for Pylos.
          Their tracks were double and monstrous
          – they would amaze anyone –
          the work of some illustrious spirit.
          At first the dark dust held
          the footprints of my cows
345   and showed them leading
          backwards into the flowering meadow.
          Then he – impossible
          as he is – himself crossed
          the sandy ground outside the path
          – but not on his feet

nor on his hands –
he had some other way
to make such monstrous tracks,
it was as though
someone had walked along
on slender planks of oak.
Now as long as he followed   350
the cattle across the sandy ground,
all the tracks showed up
very clearly in the dust.
But when he had reached the end
of the long path across the sand,
then his own tracks and the tracks
of my cows became invisible suddenly
on the hard ground.
But a mortal man noticed him
as he was driving the wide-browed cattle   355
straight towards Pylos.
So when he had shut up
the cows quietly,
he went on home
by juggling his steps
from one side of the road
to the other and then
he lay down in his cradle
as still as black night
in the gloom of that dusky cave.
Not even an eagle   360
with its sharp eye
would have spotted him.
And he rubbed his eyes
with his hands many times
while he was plotting
his crafty schemes.
Then all at once
he said carelessly:
"I haven't seen them,
I haven't heard them,

I haven't even heard
anyone talking about them.
I can't tell you about them
or win a reward for telling."'

When Phoebus Apollo had said this,
365   he sat down.

But Hermes had another tale to tell
          to the immortals,
pointing to the Son of Kronos, the leader
          of the gods.

'Father Zeus,
I will tell you the truth,
for I am infallibly honest
and don't know how to lie.
370   He came to our home
looking for his cows
with their rolling walk,
today, early,
just as the sun was rising.
He brought no witnesses
from the blessed gods,
no one who had seen anything,
but very violently
he ordered me to confess,
and he threatened many times
to hurl me down into wide Tartaros,
375   just because he possesses
the delicate flower of brilliant youth
while I was only born yesterday
– as he knows himself –
and I'm not at all
like a cattle driver,
a strong man.
Believe me – for you do claim
to be my dear father –

I didn't drive his cows home,
I didn't even
– may I be blessed –
cross over the threshold.   380
This I declare is the truth.
Helios I honour greatly,
and the other gods,
and I love you
and I dread him.
Even you know yourself
that I am not guilty.
But I will swear a great oath:
By these graceful porticoes
of the immortals! No! I didn't!
One day I will pay him back
for this cruel accusation,   385
even though he's the stronger.
But you, Zeus, help the younger.'

The Kyllenian, the Slayer of Argos, winked
as he said this, clutching his swaddling clothes
over his arm, not throwing them down.
But Zeus laughed out loud to see his mischievous
        child
denying so well, so skilfully,   390
that he knew anything about the cows.
And he ordered both of them to be of one heart
        and mind
and to search together for the cows,
but he told Hermes the guide to lead the way
and to reveal the place – without any further
        nonsense –
where he had hidden the strong cattle.
The Son of Kronos nodded his head   395
and noble Hermes obeyed him.
For the mind of Zeus who holds the aegis
persuaded him easily.

Then these two very beautiful children of Zeus
hurried away to sandy Pylos
and came to the ford of Alpheios.
They reached the fields and the high-roofed stable
400   where the animals were fed at night.
Then Hermes went inside the cave in the rock
and drove the strong cattle out into the light.
But the son of Leto, glancing around, noticed
the cowhides on the sheer rock
and at once asked glorious Hermes:

405   'You trickster,
            how were you able to cut
            the throats of two cows,
            you, a baby, only just born?
            I'm shocked myself
            to think how strong
            you'll be later on.
            You ought not to grow tall,
            Kyllenian, son of Maia!'

Apollo said this, and started twisting
tough willow shoots in his hands, intending
to bind Hermes with strong ropes.
But the ropes would not hold him
and the thongs of willow fell far away from him
410   and at once took root in the earth, there,
beneath their feet, and, intertwining
with one another, they easily tangled up
all the wild-roving cattle,
such was the will of Hermes,
he who has the mind of a thief.
Apollo watched in wonder.

Then the powerful Slayer of Argos
415   looked covertly down upon the ground,
intent on hiding his purpose, his eyes flashing fire.
But he easily soothed the son of glorious Leto,

just as he had wanted to, stern though the Archer was.
He took the lyre upon his left arm
and with the plectrum he struck each string in tune.
At the touch of his hand it resounded awesomely!   420
Phoebus Apollo laughed in delight,
for the lovely throbbing of the ineffable music
went directly to his heart and sweet longing
seized his soul as he listened.

Then the son of Maia, playing sweetly on his lyre,
took courage and stood on the left of Phoebus
        Apollo.   425
Soon, playing more clearly, he began to sing a
        prelude
– lovely the voice that came from him –
he sang of the immortal gods and the black earth,
how they came into being in the beginning,
and how they each received their allotted share of
        honour.
First among the gods he praised in song
Mnemosyne, mother of the Muses,   430
for the son of Maia belonged to her by lot.
And then all of them according to age,
the glorious son of Maia paid tribute
to all the immortal gods, singing
how each one was born, relating all things in order,
playing the lyre upon his arm.

And Apollo felt a deep and irresistible longing
lay hold on his heart and he cried out,   435
uttering winged words:

    'You scheming cattle-killer,
    you busy little friend of the feast,
    this song of yours is worth fifty cows!
    I think our differences
    will soon be settled peacefully.
    Come now, tell me this,

you ingenious son of Maia,
were you born with a talent
for this marvellous thing,
or did some deathless god
or human being give you
this great gift
and teach you divine song?
For I hear a wonderful voice
with a fresh sound
which I vow no one else
ever before has known how to make,
no man and no god
who has his home on Olympos,
no one but you, you thief,
son of Zeus and Maia.
What art is this, what muse
for inconsolable sorrows,
what skill?
Surely there are three things
to choose from and they are all here
at the same time:
joy and love and sweet sleep.
And though I'm a follower
of the Olympian Muses
who love dance
and the stately strains of song,
the swelling chant
and the thrilling tones of flutes,
never before and by nothing else
has my heart been so moved,
not even by displays of skill
at the young men's feasts.
I am filled with wonder, son of Zeus,
at the lovely way you play the lyre!

But since you have such wondrous skill,
though you are still so little,
sit down, my friend,

440

445

450

455

and respect the word
of one of your elders.
From now on you're going to have glory
among the immortal gods,
yourself and your mother too.
What I'm telling you is true.
By this shaft of cornel wood   460
I will make you the famous
and blessed guide among the gods,
and I will give you glorious gifts,
and right up to the end
I will not deceive you.'

Then Hermes answered him with artful words:

'You question me wisely, Far-Worker.
And I do not begrudge   465
introducing you to my art.
This very day you shall know it.
I want to be gentle to you
in my thoughts and in my words.
For in your heart you know
all things well.
You sit in the first place
among the deathless gods, son of Zeus,
you are brave and strong.
Wise Zeus loves you
– and it is right that he should –   470
and he has granted you glorious gifts.
They say, Far-Worker,
that from the divine voice of Zeus
you have learned the arts of prophecy
and all the divine utterances from Zeus.
And so now I wish to have a share
in all these things.
For you are free to learn
whatever you please.
But since your heart   475

moves you to play the lyre,
sing and play and give yourself to joy –
accept this from me as a gift.
And you, friend, give glory to me.
Take this clear-voiced companion
in your hands and sing well.
For you know how to express yourself
beautifully and in harmony.

480   From now on bring it light-heartedly
to the luxurious feast and the lovely dance,
even to the dazzling revels,
a joy by night and by day.
For whoever inquires of it
with skill and wisdom
and is willing to learn,
that person it teaches
through its voice
all those things

485   that delight the mind
when it is played easily
with gentle familiarity
for it shuns laborious drudgery.
But whoever, ignorant from the first,
questions it violently,
does so in vain,
the notes will be wrong
and struck in the air.
But you may learn
whatever you please.

490   So I will give you this lyre,
glorious son of Zeus.
And I, for my part, Far-Worker,
will take care of the pastures
for the wild-roving cattle on the mountain
and on the plain that feeds the horses.
So shall the cows be covered by the bulls
and they shall bring forth
both females and males abundantly.

And now there's no need for you
to be in such a violent rage,
even though you do like to win.'   495

With these words he held out the lyre.
And Phoebus Apollo received it, and willingly
handed over to Hermes his shining whip
and ordained him keeper of the cattle.
The son of Maia received it joyfully.
The glorious son of Leto, the lord, far-working
          Apollo,
took the lyre upon his left arm   500
and with the plectrum he struck each string in tune.
Under his hand it resounded awesomely,
and the god sang to it beautifully.

Then they both turned the cows back
towards the sacred meadow. But they themselves,
these two very beautiful children of Zeus,
hurried back to snowy Olympos, delighting in the
          lyre.   505
Wise Zeus was glad and made them both friends.
And Hermes loved the son of Leto continually,
even as he does now, from the proof that he gave
the lovely lyre to the Archer and taught him,
and Apollo played it skilfully upon his arm.   510
Then Hermes invented for himself the instrument
of another art: he made the pipes
whose sound can be heard from far away.
Then the Son of Leto said to Hermes:

'Son of Maia, guide,
you who are so full of tricks,
I'm afraid you might
steal the lyre back from me   515
and my curved bow at the same time.
For you have from Zeus
the honour of setting up

the business of barter among human beings
on the deeply nourishing earth.
But if you would dare to swear
the great oath of the gods
by a nod of your head
or by the potent water of Styx,
520   then you would do all I could ask
to charm and please my heart.'

So then the son of Maia nodded his head and promised
that he would never steal anything the Archer possessed
and that he would never go near his well-built house.
Then Apollo, son of Leto, nodded his head in a bond
of friendship, and promised that never
525   would there be anyone else among the immortals
whom he would love more than Hermes,
neither a god nor a man born from Zeus:

'I shall make you a perfect symbol
for the immortal gods and everyone else,
one trusted and honoured in my heart.
And I shall also give you
a marvellous wand of blessing and fortune
530   a golden one, with three branches,
which will protect you and keep you unharmed
as it accomplishes all the decrees
of noble words and deeds that I claim
to know through the voice of Zeus.
But as for that art of prophecy, my friend,
which you mentioned, child cherished by Zeus,
well, it is not lawful for you to know it,
nor for any other god either.
535   The mind of Zeus alone knows this.
I promised with a nod of my head
and I swore a strong oath
that no one apart from myself
among the ever-living gods

shall know the profound will of Zeus.
So you, brother of the golden wand,
do not ask me to reveal the divine secrets   540
which far-seeing Zeus contemplates.

As for human beings, I shall harm one
and help another, greatly bewildering
the unenviable tribes of the human race.
Yet some shall profit from my oracular voice.
Those who come guided by the cry
and the flights of prophetic birds,
these people shall be blessed by my voice.
I shall not deceive them.   545
But those who trust in birds
that just twitter vainly
and want to question my oracles against my will,
in order to know more than the ever-living gods,
these people, I say, will come on a wasted journey.
Even so I shall accept their gifts.

But I'll tell you something else,   550
son of all-glorious Maia and Zeus who holds the
        aegis,
you genius of the gods and bringer of luck.
There are certain holy ones, sisters born,
maidens adorned with swift wings,
three of them. Their heads are sprinkled over
with white barley meal and they make their homes
under the cliffs of Parnassos.   555
They taught divination apart from me,
the art which I used to practise
around my cattle while still a boy.
My father took no notice.
From their home they fly, now here,
now there, feeding on honeycomb
and bringing all things to pass.
And when they have eaten of the golden honey   560

they are inspired and want to speak the truth
graciously. But if they are deprived
of the sweet food of the gods
they tell you lies, swarming
to and fro among one another.
These, then, I give you.
Inquire of them sincerely
565   and delight your heart.
And if you come across some mortal,
he will often hear your voice
if he is lucky.
Take these things, son of Maia,
and look after the wild-roving cattle
with twisted horns and the horses
and mules who have so much to endure.'

570   And Zeus decreed that over lions with flashing eyes
and boars with gleaming tusks and dogs
and all those sheep which the broad earth nourishes
– over all the flocks –
glorious Hermes should be lord,
and that he should be the only
consecrated messenger to Hades,
who, though receiving no gift for himself,
will yet give Hermes no mean prize.

So the lord Apollo came to love the son of Maia
575   with every gesture of friendship.
And the Son of Kronos gave him grace as well.
Now he mingles with everyone, mortals and immortals
            alike.
A few he helps, but he endlessly beguiles
the race of human beings in the darkness of the night.

And so farewell, son of Zeus and Maia.
580   And now I shall remember you and another song too.

V

HYMN TO APHRODITE

Muse, speak to me of the works of Aphrodite,
the golden one, the Cyprian,
she who awakens sweet longing in the gods
and subdues the race of human beings
and the birds that fly through the air
and all the wild beasts and the many creatures
that the dry land feeds, that the sea nourishes.   5
All these love what she brings to pass,
the Cytherean in her lovely crown.

But there are three hearts
she can neither persuade nor beguile.
First, there is the daughter of Zeus who holds the
      aegis,
Athena with her gleaming eyes.
The works of golden Aphrodite give her no pleasure,
she likes wars and the work of Ares,   10
fights and battles and caring for her glorious crafts.
She was the first to teach the craftsmen of the earth
how to make carriages and chariots patterned with
      bronze.
She it is who teaches soft-skinned maidens
the wondrous arts of the home,
putting them in the mind of each one.   15

The second goddess whom laughter-loving Aphrodite
cannot tame in love is Artemis
with her golden arrows and her hunting cries.

She loves the bow and slaying wild animals
in the mountains, she loves lyres and dancing
and the piercing cries of women,

20   shadowy glades and the cities of just men.

The third one who is not charmed by the works of
      Aphrodite
is Hestia, the pure maiden, who was the first-born,
the oldest child of crafty Kronos,
and also the youngest, the last-born,
by the will of Zeus who holds the aegis.
Poseidon and Apollo courted her, the mighty goddess,
but she was wholly unwilling and adamantly refused

25   them.
And she swore a great oath – which has been fulfilled –
touching the head of father Zeus who holds the aegis,
that she would be virgin all her days, divine goddess.
So instead of marriage, father Zeus gave her a lovely
      gift

30   and now she sits at the heart of the home,
accepting the prize of all the offerings.
She is honoured in all the temples of the gods
and she is the goddess most revered among all the
      mortals.

These are the three hearts
Aphrodite can neither persuade nor beguile.
But no one else, none of the blessed gods

35   or human beings, can ever escape Aphrodite.
She has even led astray the mind of thunder-loving
      Zeus,
even though he is the greatest of all
and has the greatest honour.
The truth is, she beguiled his discreet heart
whenever she pleased, uniting him easily
with mortal women and making him utterly forget

40   Hera, his sister and wife, the most beautiful
among the deathless goddesses.

She is the most glorious of goddesses
whom crafty Kronos and mother Rhea bore,
and Zeus, whose knowledge is incorruptible,
made her his respected wife in all her wisdom.

But Zeus in turn cast sweet longing   45
to be united with a mortal man
into the heart of Aphrodite herself
so that, very soon, not even she should be able
to keep away from the bed of a mortal man
lest she, who loves laughter, should one day
sweetly smile upon the whole company of gods
and, mocking them all, say
that she had mated gods with mortal women   50
who had borne mortal sons to immortal gods
and she had also mated goddesses with mortal men.

So it was for Anchises who was tending his cattle
on the high mountains of Ida with its many springs
that Zeus put sweet longing in her heart
– he who looked in form like a god.   55
And when she saw him she loved him,
Aphrodite, lover of laughter,
and a terrible passion seized her heart.

She went away to Cyprus and she entered
her fragrant temple at Paphos where she has
her sanctuary and fragrant altar.
There she went inside and closed   60
the shining doors behind her.
There the Graces bathed her and anointed her
with heavenly oils, the kind the eternal gods always
        use,
divinely sweet and filled with fragrance.
And laughter-loving Aphrodite
put on all her beautiful clothes   65
and adorned herself with gold,
then she hurried away to Troy,

leaving sweet-smelling Cyprus behind
and, making a path high up through the clouds,
she passed swiftly between them.

So she came to Ida with its many springs,
the mother of the wild animals,
and she went straight over the mountain
to the sheepfolds. Behind her moved
70   grey wolves, fawning on her,
and bright-eyed lions and bears
and swift-footed leopards, ravenous for deer.
She felt joy in her heart to see them
and she filled their hearts with longing
so that they all went in twos
into the shade of the valleys
and made love with each other.

75   She came to the well-built huts
and found him in the stable,
Anchises, the hero, left all alone,
away from the others,
he who had the beauty of the gods.
The others were following their cattle
through the grasslands, all of them
except him, he was in the stable,
left all alone, away from the others,
80   walking up and down and playing his lyre thrillingly.

She stood before him,
Aphrodite, daughter of Zeus,
in form and stature like a pure maiden,
lest he recognize her with his eyes and be afraid.
Anchises saw her and marvelled at her,
85   astonished at her form and shape and shining clothes.
She wore a robe more brilliant than the radiance of fire,
She had twisted bracelets and earrings glistening
like flowers and wondrously beautiful necklaces
lay around her soft throat,

lovely and golden and finely patterned
and they shimmered over her delicate breasts
like the moon – a wonder to see.   90

Love seized Anchises
and he spoke to her these words:
'Greetings, Lady, whoever you are
of the blessed gods who have come to my house.
Is it Artemis or Leto or golden Aphrodite,
or noble Themis or bright-eyed Athena?
Or perhaps you are one of the Graces   95
coming to visit me here, one of those
who keep company with all the gods
and are called immortal?
Or perhaps you are one of the Nymphs
who haunt the beautiful woods
or even one of the Nymphs
who live in this beautiful mountain
in the springs of the rivers and the grassy meadows?
On a mountain peak, somewhere that can be seen   100
from all around, I will make you an altar
and I will offer you wonderful sacrifices in every
      season.
And you, out of the kindness of your heart,
let me be a splendid man among the Trojans.
Make my children strong in the time that is to come.
As for myself, may I for a long time live well   105
and see the light of the sun, blessed among my
      people,
so may I reach the threshold of old age.'

Then Aphrodite, daughter of Zeus, answered him:

'Anchises, most glorious of men born on earth,
I am no goddess. Why do you see me
as one of the immortals? No, I am a mortal,
and my mother was a mortal woman.   110
Otreus is my father, his name is famous

– perhaps you have heard of him? –
he rules over the whole of Phrygia with its fortified
        hills.
Yet I know your language as well as I know my own.
For the nurse who brought me up at home was Trojan.
115   She took me from my dear mother
        while I was still a tiny child
        and she cared for me devotedly.
        That's why I know your language as well as I know
                my own.
        But now the Slayer of Argos with his golden wand
        has carried me away from the dances of Artemis,
        the huntress with the golden arrows who calls so
                loudly.
120   We were playing, many of us, nymphs and maidens
        who bring in many oxen, and a great throng of people
        was circling around us when the Slayer of Argos
        with his golden wand captured me.
        He carried me over many fields ploughed by mortals,
        and over many lands which nobody owns
        and nobody cares for, where wild beasts roam
        through shadowed valleys, eating raw flesh.
125   And I thought I would never again
        touch the life-giving earth with my feet.
        And he told me that I should be called
        the lawful wife of Anchises in the bridal bed
        and should bear you wonderful children.
        But when he had shown me this and counselled me,
        the strong Slayer of Argos went away,
        back to the tribes of the immortal gods.
130   And so I have come to you
        – unyielding necessity is upon me.

        But I entreat you, by Zeus and by your noble parents
        – for no base people could bear a son like you –
        take me as I am, untouched and innocent of love,
        and show me to your father and your wise mother
135   and to your brothers, born from the same womb.

I shall be no unworthy daughter for them, but
    worthy.
Quickly, send a messenger
to the Phrygians with their swift horses
and tell my father and my sorrowing mother.
They will send you heaps of gold and woven
    garments,
and you – you accept their splendid gifts as a
    dowry.   140
And then, after you have done all these things,
make ready the marriage feast that excites love
and is honourable in the eyes of mortals and the
    immortal gods.'

The goddess, speaking like this,
filled his heart with sweet longing.
So love seized Anchises and he spoke these words:

'If you are really mortal   145
and the mother who gave you birth was a woman
and Otreus with the famous name is your father
– as you say – and if you come here
by the will of Hermes, the immortal guide,
then you shall be called my wife for ever,
and no one, no god or human being,
will stop me from making love to you   150
immediately, right now,
not even if Apollo himself, the Archer,
were to hurl his deadly arrows from his silver bow.
Woman, so like a goddess,
I would willingly go down to the house of Hades
once I had lain upon your bed.'
Saying this, he took her hand.   155
And laughter-loving Aphrodite turned her face
    away
and casting her beautiful eyes down
she glided to the bed strewn with rugs,

already laid with soft coverings for its lord,
the skins of bears and deep-roaring lions
160   which he had slain himself high up in the mountains.

And when they had lain down upon the well-made
        bed,
Anchises first took from her body her glistening
        jewels,
brooches and curved bracelets and earrings and
        necklaces.
Then he unfastened her girdle and took off
her shining clothes and placed them
165   on a silver-studded chair. And then,
by the will of the gods and destiny,
he lay with her, a mortal man
with an immortal goddess – not knowing what he did.

At the hour when the shepherds turn their oxen
and their strong sheep back from the flowering
        meadows
towards the stables, then it was that Aphrodite
170   poured upon Anchises a sweet deep sleep
but clothed her own body in beautiful clothes.
And when the divine goddess had fully clothed her body
she stood in the hut and her head
touched the well-made roof.
Unearthly beauty shone from her cheeks,
175   such as belongs to the Cytherean in her lovely crown.
Then she woke him from sleep and she spoke these
        words:

'Arise, son of Dardanos! Why do you sleep so deeply?
Now think, do I appear to you to be the same
as when you first saw me with your eyes?'

She spoke. He heard her and started from sleep
180   abruptly.
When he saw the neck and the beautiful eyes

of Aphrodite, he felt dread and turned his eyes aside.
He covered his own beautiful face with his cloak
and entreated her, uttering winged words:

'Goddess, the moment I first saw you with my eyes   185
I knew you were divine.
But you did not tell me the truth.
On my knees I beg you, by Zeus who holds the aegis,
don't let me live a crippled life among human beings,
but pity me. For when a man has slept with
an immortal goddess he loses his powers.'   190

Then Aphrodite, daughter of Zeus, answered him:

'Anchises, most glorious of mortals, have courage.
Let not your heart be so afraid.
There is no need to fear,
you will not suffer harm from me
nor from the other blessed ones,   195
for you are loved by the gods.
You shall have a dear son
who will rule among the Trojans
and children will be born
to his children forever.
Aeneas shall be his name
because my anguish was so dreadful
that I fell into the bed of a mortal man.
Yet of all human beings those of your race   200
are always closest to the gods
in their beauty and their form.

It was for his beauty that wise Zeus carried off
golden-haired Ganymede to live among the
        immortals
and to pour wine for the gods in the house of Zeus
– a wonder to see – and he is honoured by all the
        gods,   205
drawing the red nectar from a golden bowl.

But endless sorrow gripped the heart of Tros
for he did not know where the divine whirlwind
had swept away his dear son.
He mourned for him continually, every day,
210   and Zeus took pity on him and gave him,
as a recompense for his son, prancing horses,
the same ones that carry the immortal gods.
He gave them as a gift for him to keep.
Then, at the command of Zeus, the Slayer of Argos,
the guide, told him everything, how his son
would be immortal and ageless like the gods.
215   When he heard this message from Zeus
he wept no more and was glad in his heart
and he rode joyfully on his horses
whose feet are like storms.

So, too, golden-throned Dawn snatched away
        Tithonos,
another of your race who was like the gods.
And she went to ask the Son of Kronos in his dark
220   clouds
to make him immortal and let him live forever.
Zeus nodded and her wish was fulfilled.
Foolish one, Dawn, the queen, did not think
in her heart to ask for youth for him
and to have deadly old age smoothed away.
225   So as long as lovely youth possessed him
he lived in rapture with early-born and golden-throned
        Dawn
by the streams of Ocean at the ends of the earth.
But when the first grey hairs began to flow down
from his beautiful head and well-bearded chin,
230   then Dawn, the queen, stayed away from his bed
though she took care of him in her house,
giving him food and ambrosia and fine clothes.
But when hateful old age weighed him down
        completely
so that he could neither move nor lift his limbs,

then this was the plan that seemed best in her heart: 235
she laid him in a chamber and shut its shining doors.
His voice flows on endlessly, but the strength has gone
which once was his when his limbs were supple.

I would not want you to be deathless among the
        deathless gods
and to live like that for ever.   240
But if you were to live on as you are now,
in your looks and your body, and be called my
        husband,
then sorrow would never veil my cautious heart.
As it is, old age will soon enfold you,
remorseless, the same for everyone,   245
for it stands one day at the side of all human beings,
deadly, dispiriting – even the gods abhor it.
As for me, there will be great shame
among the immortal gods, endlessly,
all my days, because of you.
Up until now they were afraid of my love affairs
and my wiles since, sooner or later,
I mated all the immortal gods with mortal women.   250
My mind overruled them all. But now
I shall not dare to open my mouth
on these matters among the immortals
because I fell into a very great madness,
miserable, unspeakable,
I went out of my mind,
conceiving a child beneath my girdle,   255
sleeping with a mortal man.

As for the child, as soon as he first sees
the light of the sun, the deep-breasted
mountain Nymphs will nourish him,
those who live on this great and holy mountain.
They do not share the nature of mortals or
        immortals.
They live a long time and eat ambrosial food   260

and they dance the beautiful dance of the immortals.
The Sileni and the sharp-eyed Slayer of Argos
make love with them in the far depths of their lovely
    caves.
When they are born, pines and towering oaks spring up
265   at the same time out of the earth that nourishes mortals
   – beautiful, luxuriant trees, growing on the high
    mountains.
They stand very tall and are called
the sacred places of the immortals.
Mortals never cut them down with an axe.
But when the destiny of death approaches,
270   those beautiful trees, they first dry up in the earth
and then the bark shrivels up around them,
the branches fall away and at last
the soul of the tree and the soul of the Nymph
leave the light of the sun together.

These Nymphs will keep my son and bring him up with
    them.
And when the lovely prime of youth first possesses him,
the goddesses will bring him here and show you your
275   child.
And when you see him with your eyes
– like a young shoot –
you will delight in looking at him
for he will look most like a god.
280   Then you shall take him at once to wind-swept Ilion.
And if any human being ever asks you who was the
    mother
who conceived your dear son beneath her girdle,
remember to repeat this story the way I tell you:
"He is the son, they say, of a flower-like Nymph,
one of those who live here
285   on this mountain covered with forests."
But if you ever mention it, carelessly boasting
how you made love with the rich-crowned Cytherean,
then Zeus will be enraged and hurl

a smoking thunderbolt at you.
And now I have told you everything.
But you, hold this in your mind.
Do not let yourself call me by name.   290
Beware the wrath of the gods.'

With these words she soared up into windy heaven.

Farewell, goddess, queen of Cyprus with its fine
    buildings.
I began with you and now I shall turn to another
    song.

VI

HYMN TO APHRODITE

Reverend
golden-crowned
beautiful Aphrodite
I shall sing,
she who possesses the heights
of all
sea-wet Cyprus
where Zephyros swept her
with his moist breath
over the waves
of the roaring sea
in soft foam.

In their diadems of gold
5   the Hours joyously
received her
and wrapped
the ambrosial garments around her.
On her immortal head
they laid a crown of gold
that was wonderfully made
and in
the pierced lobes of her ears
they hung
flowers of copper
from the mountains
and precious gold.
10   Round her delicate throat
and her silvery breasts

they fastened
necklaces of gold
which they,
the gold-filleted Hours,
wear themselves
when they go
to the lovely dances of the gods
in their father's house.

And then,
when they had arranged
all these decorations
on her body,
they led her   15
to the immortal gods
who saw her
and welcomed her
and reached out their hands
towards her

longing,
every one of them,
to take her home
to be his lawful wife,
so enraptured
were they all
with the beauty of the Cytherean
in her crown of violets.

Farewell,
quick-glancing
honey-sweet goddess.
Grant me victory   20
in this contest,
favour my song.

And now I shall remember you
and another song too.

VII

HYMN TO DIONYSOS

Dionysos
I will call to mind,
son of glorious Semele.

How he appeared
on a shore of the desolate sea,
there, where the cliffs jut out,
looking like a young man
in the flower of youth.

Rich dark hair flowed round him,
a purple robe hung down
from his strong shoulders.

Suddenly there were pirates, Tyrrhenians,
they raced across the wine-dark sea,
rowing their ship with many oars.
A destiny of doom drove them.

When they saw him
they nodded
to each other
and instantly
they leapt out
and caught him
and shoved him
into their ship,
thrilled and elated,

5

10

imagining him
the son
of those kings
gods love.

With harsh ropes
they wanted
to hold him down.

But the ropes would not hold.
The willow bonds
just dropped off him,
fell far away from his hands and feet.

He sat there
and his dark eyes smiled.

Then the helmsman knew.   15
At once he cried out,
called to his comrades:

'Madmen!
Who is this god
you have seized and bound
– he is so strong –
not even our well-built ship
can carry him?

Either this is Zeus
or silver-bowed Apollo
or else it is Poseidon.   20
He has not the look
of a mortal man,
he is like the gods
who live on Olympos.
Come, let us set him free
straightaway
on this dark shore.

Don't lay hands on him
lest he fly into a rage
and rouse up terrible winds
and huge storms.'

25   He said this, but the master
reproved him
with these hateful words:

'Madman yourself,
watch the wind,
haul the sail,
hold fast
to all the ship's ropes,
as for him,
we men will deal with him.
I expect
he's heading for Egypt
or Cyprus or the Hyperboreans
or even farther away
30   but in the end he'll tell us
all about his friends and his possessions
and his brothers.
Some god sent him to us.'

He said this, and he set
the ship's mast and the sail
and the wind swelled
into the middle of the sail
and on either side
the crew stretched the ropes tight.

Suddenly
wonderful things appeared among them.

35   First of all
wine burst out bubbling,

sweet fragrant wine
streamed all over the swift ship
and a heavenly smell floated up.
When they saw it
all the sailors were amazed.

Suddenly a vine
sprang up the sail
to the top,
spreading out both ways,
and grapes hung down
in clusters
all over it
and a dark ivy   40
curled
around the mast
blossoming with flowers
and sprouting
lovely berries

and suddenly
all the rowlocks grew garlands.

When they saw this
at last
they cried to the helmsman
to take the ship in to land.

But then the god
turned into a lion
inside the ship, terrible,
on the highest part,   45
and roared loudly.

And amidships he made a bear
with a shaggy neck
– revealing his portents –

and it stood up threateningly,
and on the top deck the lion
glared furiously.

Everyone was terrified,
they ran to the stern
in a panic
and huddled
round the helmsman,
50   the man with the wise soul.

But the lion suddenly sprang
and seized the master.

When they saw it
they all
– longing to escape
such a dreadful doom –
they all leapt
overboard together
into the brilliant sea
and became
dolphins.

But the helmsman was saved.
The god had mercy on him
and made him truly happy.
He said to him:

55   'Courage, my god-like friend,
you have charmed my heart.
I am Dionysos,
the roaring god.
My mother was Semele,
daughter of Cadmus,
and she bore me
after she lay in love with Zeus.'

Farewell,
child of Semele
with the beautiful face.
Anyone who forgets you
forgets
how to compose
sweet song.

VIII

HYMN TO ARES

Supremely strong Ares,
golden-helmeted chariot-rider,
tough-hearted, shield-carrying
guardian of cities,
bronze in armour, brave of hand,
the tireless, spear-sharp
rampart of Olympos,
father of war-winning Victory,
the ally of Themis.

5   You are a tyrant to the rebellious,
a leader to the most just,
you carry the staff of manhood,
you whirl your disc of bright fire across the sky
among the seven tracks of the constellations
where blazing horses bear you forever
beyond the third orbit.

Hear me, helper of mortals,
whose gift is the courage of youth.
10   From high above, shine down upon our lives
your gentle light and your warrior's power,
so I may drive away bitter cowardice from my head
and subdue my soul's beguiling impulse,
so may I restrain the shrill rage in my heart
15   which excites me to charge
into the chilling din of battle.

Rather, blessed god, give me the courage
to stand my ground within the safe laws of peace,
shunning hostility and hatred
and the fate of a violent death.

IX

HYMN TO ARTEMIS

Sing, Muse, of Artemis,
sister of the archer god,
the maiden who delights in arrows
who grew up with Apollo.

By Meles, where the reeds are deep,
she harnesses her horses
and swiftly through Smyrna
she speeds her chariot
all in gold

to Klaros, the vine land,
where Apollo sits waiting
with his silver bow

for Artemis
who delights in arrows
and lets them fly from far away.

And so I greet you
and all the other goddesses
with this song.

You are my first song,
with you I begin,
and now I have begun with you
I shall turn to another song.

X

HYMN TO APHRODITE

I shall sing of the Cytherean
born in Cyprus

who gives such gentle gifts
to mortals.

Her lovely face is always smiling
and lovely is the bloom that plays upon it.

I greet you, goddess,

Queen of Salamis
with its strong buildings,

Queen of Cyprus
set in the sea.

Grant me an enchanting song.

And now I shall remember you
and another song too.

5

XI

HYMN TO ATHENA

Pallas Athena I begin to sing,
guardian of the city,
the formidable goddess.

With Ares she cares for the work of war,
the destruction of cities
and the shouts of battle.

It is she who watches over the people,
when they go out to war
and when they come back.

5   Farewell, goddess,
grant me good fortune
and happiness too.

XII

HYMN TO HERA

Hera I sing
on her golden throne.

Her mother was Rhea.

She is queen of the immortal gods,
she is pre-eminent in beauty,
she is the sister of thundering Zeus,
she is also his wife.

She is the glorious one.

All the blessed gods
on vast Olympos
are in awe of her.

They honour her equally with Zeus   5
who loves thunder and lightning.

XIII

HYMN TO DEMETER

Demeter with her lovely hair,
sacred goddess,

I begin to sing
of her and her daughter,
the surpassingly beautiful
Persephone.

Farewell, goddess.
Save our city
and guide my song.

XIV

HYMN TO THE MOTHER
OF THE GODS

Mother of all the gods
and all mortals

Sing of her
for me, Muse,
daughter of mighty Zeus,
a clear song.

She loves
the clatter of rattles
the din of kettle drums

and she loves
the wailing of flutes

and also she loves
the howling of wolves
and the growling
of bright-eyed lions

echoing hills
and wooded hollows.

And so farewell, goddess,
I greet you
and all the other goddesses
with my song.

XV

HYMN TO HERAKLES, THE
LION-HEARTED

Herakles, son of Zeus,
shall be my song.

He is the greatest man on the whole earth.

Alkmene gave birth to him in Thebes,
city of the beautiful dances.
The Son of Kronos made love to her
shrouded in his dark clouds.

Once he wandered over the unutterably vast
earth and across the sea.
Lord Eurystheus told him to.

He did many reckless things himself
and he suffered just as many too.

But now it is different.
He lives in a beautiful home
in snowy Olympos, enjoying himself.
He has Hebe with him as well
and she has such lovely ankles.

Greetings, lord, son of Zeus.
Give me virtue and prosperity.

XVI

HYMN TO ASKLEPIOS

Asklepios, healer of sickness,
I begin to sing, son of Apollo.

Divine Koronis, daughter of King Phlegyas,
gave birth to him in the fields of Dotion.

For human beings he is a source of great joy,
he charms bitter pains away from them.

And so farewell to you, lord.   5
My song to you is my prayer.

XVII

HYMN TO THE DIOSKOUROI

Sing, Muse,
in your clear voice.

Sing of Castor and Pollux,
the Tyndaridai,
who were born
from Olympian Zeus.

The noble Leda
gave birth to them
under the peak
of Mount Taygetos

when secretly
she yielded
to the Son of Kronos
in his black clouds.

5   Greetings, Tyndaridai,
riders on swift horses.

XVIII

HYMN TO HERMES

Hermes of Kyllene
I sing,

the Slayer of Argos,
lord of Kyllene and Arcadia,
the land of sheep.

He is the messenger of the gods,
he brings luck.

His mother was Maia,
daughter of Atlas,

the shy goddess
who lay in love with Zeus.

She shunned the crowd
of the blessed gods,
she lived in a shadowy cave,

and there
in the depths of night
the Son of Kronos
made love to the nymph
with the beautiful hair

while sweet sleep
held

5

the white arms
of Hera.

And nobody noticed,
not the immortal gods
nor human beings.

10   Greetings to you,
son of Zeus and Maia.
I began my song
with you
and now I will turn
to another song.

Farewell, Hermes,
you give grace,
you are the guide,
you give us good things.

XIX

HYMN TO PAN

Muse,
speak to me of the loved child
of Hermes

with his goat's feet
and his two horns

the one who loves noise

who roams about
in wooded meadows
together with
dancing nymphs who tread upon

peaks of rock
even goats leave bare,
calling out

Pan

god of shepherds
dust-parched
with dazzling hair

who has
all the snowy crests
and the mountain ridges
and the rocky paths

for his home.

Here and there
he roams
through dense thickets
and sometimes
he is drawn
to soft streams
and sometimes
10   he wanders back
over precipices of rock
climbing
up to the
highest peak
to watch over his sheep.

Often he runs along
shining distant mountains
and often
he races down
the mountain sides
killing wild beasts,
so piercing is his eye.

Only in the evening
when he lets go the hunt
15   then he makes sounds
on his pipes of reed
playing a sweet deep song.

And no bird
can surpass him
in song

not even she who
when Spring is full of flowers
pours forth her lament

among the leaves
singing with honey voice
a mournful song.

Then the clear-singing
mountain nymphs
roam around with him
on their strong feet   20
chanting by a spring
of dark water

while Echo
on the mountain-top
wails.

The god

now this
side of the chorus
now that

or at times
gliding
into the midst of them

conducts the dancing feet

wearing the blood-red
skin of a lynx
upon his back

his heart
delighting in
the shrill songs
in a soft meadow   25

where crocuses
and sweet-smelling hyacinths
mix in with the grass
wherever they like.

They sing of the blessed gods
and high Olympos
they tell of Hermes
who brings luck
beyond all others
how he is the swift messenger
of all the gods

30   and how he came to Arcadia
with its many springs
mother of the flocks
where Kyllene is
the sacred place
of the god.

And there
though he was a god
he tended the sheep
with their shaggy fleece
for a mortal man

all because

there came over him
and intensified

melting longing

to lie with
the nymph with the beautiful hair,
daughter of Dryops.

35   It ended in a joyous marriage.

And in the house she gave birth
to a dear son for Hermes
who from the first
was marvellous to look upon

with goat's feet
and two horns,
loving noise
and laughing sweetly.

But his mother jumped up
and ran away.

As soon as she
caught sight of
his harsh face
and his thick beard
she was terrified
and left the child alone.

Quickly Hermes   40
who brings the luck
took him in his arms
accepting him

and happy in his heart
beyond measure
was the god.

So quickly
wrapping his son
in the warm skins
of mountain hares

he went to the home
of the immortal gods
and he sat down
beside Zeus and the other gods

45   and showed them his boy.

                    Then all the immortal gods
                    were glad in their hearts
                    but most of all
                    Bacchos Dionysos.

                    They called him

                    Pan

                    because he delighted
                    the hearts
                    of all.

                    And so to you lord
                    farewell
                    I would please you
                    with my song.

              And now I shall remember you
              and another song too.

XX

HYMN TO HEPHAISTOS

Sing, Muse,
in a clear voice,
sing of Hephaistos
who is famous for his skill.

With Athena of the gleaming eyes,
he taught human beings
all over the earth
their glorious crafts,

people who before
used to live in caves
in the mountains
like wild beasts.

But now they have learned   5
how to make crafts
from Hephaistos
who is famous for his art.

Now they have an easy life
the whole year round,
living in their own homes
at peace.

But be gracious, Hephaistos.
Grant me virtue
and prosperity too.

XXI

HYMN TO APOLLO

Phoebus,
it is of you
the swan sings clearly,

his wings beating,

swooping down to the shore
of the whirling river Peneios.

And it is of you
the poet sings,

speaking sweetly
to his clear-voiced lyre.

At the beginning
and at the end

it is always of you.

And so farewell to you, lord,
I seek your grace with my song.

XXII

HYMN TO POSEIDON

Poseidon
the great god
I begin to sing,
he who moves the earth
and the desolate sea

the deep water god

who is lord
of Helikon
and broad Aigai.

Shaker of the Earth
the gods gave you
a double honour.

You are
the tamer of horses
and the saviour of ships.

Farewell, Poseidon,
you hold up the earth.

You are dark-haired
you are blessed
you have a kind heart.

Help those who sail upon the sea
in ships.

5

XXIII

HYMN TO THE SON OF
KRONOS, MOST HIGH

Zeus I shall sing,
the best of the gods
and the greatest.

He sees all,
he rules all,
he accomplishes all things.

He converses wisely with Themis,
the goddess who sits
leaning towards him.

Be gracious,
Son of Kronos,
who sees everything.

You are the most famous,
the greatest
of all.

XXIV

HYMN TO HESTIA

Hestia,
you are the one
who takes care of the holy house
in sacred Pytho, the house
of the archer lord Apollo,

soft oil
flowing forth from your hair.

Come into this house,
come, having one heart
with wise Zeus,   5

and be gracious to my song too.

XXV

HYMN TO THE MUSES AND APOLLO

May I begin with the Muses
and with Apollo
and with Zeus.

It is because
of the Muses
and the archer Apollo

that there exist on the earth
people who sing songs
and play the lyre.

Kings come from Zeus.

If the Muses love you
then you are blessed
and sweet sound

flows from your mouth.

Greetings,
children of Zeus,
and give honour to my song.

And now I shall remember you
and another song too.

XXVI

HYMN TO DIONYSOS

Ivy-haired
loud-roaring
Dionysos

I begin to sing

the brilliant son
of Zeus and glorious Semele.

The nymphs
with their lovely hair
took him from his father,
the lord,
and held him to their breasts
and nourished him tenderly
in the valleys of Nysa.   5

The cave smelt sweet
where he grew
by the grace of his father
to be counted among the immortals.

But when the goddesses
had finished caring for him,
this god
who has hymns sung to him everywhere,

then he started
ceaselessly
wandering

roaming
all over the woods and valleys,
ivy wreaths and laurel
twining thickly
round him,
nymphs
following
wherever he went
– he was their leader –
till noise
possessed
the whole
unspeakably vast
forest.

And so farewell to you,
Dionysos,
with your ripe clustering
grapes.

Grant us to come back again
joyously at this season,
and from this season onwards
for many years to come.

XXVII

HYMN TO ARTEMIS

Artemis I sing
with her golden arrows
and her hunting cry,
sacred virgin,
deer-huntress
showering arrows,
sister of Apollo
with his golden sword.

In mountains of shadow
and peaks of wind
she delights in the chase,
she arches her bow
of solid gold

she lets fly
arrows
that moan.

Crests
of high mountains
tremble,
the forest
in darkness
screams
with the terrible howling
of wild animals

the earth itself shudders,
even the sea
alive with fish.

But the heart of the goddess
is strong,
she darts everywhere
in and out, every way,
killing
the race of wild beasts.

And when she has had enough
of looking for animals,
this huntress
who takes pleasure in arrows,
when her heart is elated,
then she unstrings
her curved bow

and goes
to the great house
of Phoebus Apollo,
her dear brother,
to the rich land
of Delphi,
and there she arranges
the lovely dances
of the Muses and Graces.

There she hangs up
her unstrung bow
and her quiver of arrows
and gracefully
clothing her body
she takes first place
and leads them
in the dance.

With heavenly voices
they all sing.

They sing of Leto
with her lovely ankles,
how she gave birth
to the best children
of all the gods,
supreme
in what they say
and do.

Farewell,
children of Zeus and Leto
with her beautiful hair.

And now I shall remember you
and another song too.

XXVIII

HYMN TO ATHENA

Pallas Athena I begin to sing,
the glorious goddess with gleaming eyes,
brilliantly inventive, her heart relentless,
the formidable maiden, guardian of cities,
the courageous Tritogeneia.

Wise Zeus gave birth to her himself
out of his majestic head.
Golden armour clothed her,
it was glistening, war-like.
All the gods who saw her
were overcome with awe.

Suddenly she was there
before Zeus who holds the aegis.
She sprang from his immortal head
shaking her sharp spear.
Great Olympos trembled terribly
at the power of the goddess
with the gleaming eyes.

And the earth screamed awfully
all around her and the sea
started to move, frothing
with dark waves and suddenly
the salt sea stopped.

The brilliant son of Hyperion
stilled
his swift-footed horses
for a long time until

Pallas Athena, the maiden,   15
unclasped the heavenly armour
from her immortal shoulders.
Wise Zeus was delighted.

Farewell, daughter of Zeus
who holds the aegis.
And now I shall remember you
and another song too.

XXIX

HYMN TO HESTIA

Hestia, you hold
the highest honour,
you have a seat forever
in the lofty houses
of all the immortal gods
and all the people
who walk upon the earth.
Your gift is the beautiful one,
the gift of honour.

Without you
5 mortals could have no feasts,
no one can begin,
if the first
and the last drink
of the honey sweet wine
is not offered to Hestia.

And you, too, Slayer of Argos,
son of Zeus and Maia,
you are the messenger
of the blessed gods,
you carry the golden wand,
you give good things.
10 Be gracious and help us,
together with Hestia,
she who is dear
and deserving of reverence.

For you both live in the beautiful homes
of people who live on earth
and who wish to be friends with one another,
and you follow good deeds
with wisdom and strength.

Farewell, daughter of Kronos,
and you too, Hermes,
with your golden wand.
And now I shall remember you
and another song too.

XXX

HYMN TO GAIA, MOTHER OF ALL

Gaia, mother of all,
I shall sing,
the strong foundation, the oldest one.
She feeds everything in the world.

Whoever walks upon her sacred ground
or moves through the sea
or flies in the air, it is she
who nourishes them from her treasure-store.

5   Queen of Earth, through you
beautiful children,
beautiful harvests,
come.

It is you who give life to mortals
and who take life away.
Blessed is the one you honour with a willing heart.
He who has this has everything.

His fields thicken with life-giving corn,
10   his cattle grow heavy in the pastures,
his house brims over with good things.
The men are masters of their city,

the laws are just,
the women are fair,
great riches and fortune follow them.
Their sons delight in the ecstasy of youth,

their daughters play
in dances garlanded with flowers,
they skip happily on the grass   15
over soft flowers.

It was you who honoured them,
sacred goddess, generous spirit.
Farewell, mother of the gods,
bride of starry Heaven.

For my song, allow me a life
my heart loves.
And now I shall remember you
and another song too.

XXXI

HYMN TO HELIOS

Helios, the blazing Sun,
sing of him, Muse, Kalliope,
daughter of Zeus,

how he was born
to ox-eyed Euryphaessa
and the son of Gaia and starry Ouranos.

Hyperion it was
who married glorious Euryphaessa,
his own sister,
and she gave birth
to beautiful children,

Eos with arms of rose,
Selene with lovely hair,
and Helios who never wearies.

He is like the gods.

Riding his chariot of horses
he shines down upon all things,
on mortals and immortal gods the same.

His eyes gleam terribly
beneath his golden helmet.

Bright rays flash from him
brilliantly, and from
his temples the bright

cheek-pieces around his head
enclose his lovely face
which shines from far away.

A beautiful fine-spun robe
glows on his skin
and shimmers in the wind
while stallions carry him.

But then he stills
his horses, stays
the golden yoke   15
of his chariot until

again, wondrously,
he drives them down
through heaven to Ocean.

Farewell, lord,
freely grant me
a life my heart loves.

And now I have begun with you
I shall celebrate the race of beings
with the power of speech

who are half-divine
and whose works have been shown
to mortals by the Muses.

XXXII

HYMN TO SELENE

Selene, sing of her,
Muses with your sweet voices,
daughters of Zeus, Son of Kronos,
weavers of song,

Sing us the story of the long-winged Moon.

Glistening in heaven
from her immortal head,
a radiance encircles earth
and from her shining light
great beauty comes.

The air unlit before
glows with her golden crown
and her beams are bright as day

whenever Selene, the goddess

– once she has washed
her beautiful body
in the waters of Ocean
and gathered her garments
which gleam so far
and yoked together
her flashing horses,
their necks high-curving –

she speeds them eagerly on,   10
these horses,
their long manes flowing,

at evening
in the middle of the month,

when her great orb swells to the full
and her beams appear most brilliant
as there in heaven she grows and grows.

And so she becomes a pledge,
a sign for human beings.

– Once upon a time
in a marriage bed
she lay in love
with the Son of Kronos
and she conceived   15
and gave birth
to a daughter, Pandia,
who was unusually beautiful
among the immortal gods –

Queen, farewell,
goddess with white arms,
divine Selene,
the kindly goddess
whose hair shimmers.

You were my first song
and now I shall sing the fame
of those mortals who are half-divine,

whose works poets honour
out of their lovely mouths,
poets who are only servants of the Muses.   20

XXXIII

HYMN TO THE DIOSKOUROI

Muses with your glancing eyes,
sing to us of the Sons of Zeus,
the Tyndaridai,
glorious children of Leda
whose ankles are so beautiful.
There is Castor who tames horses
and Pollux who is without blame.

5 Under the peak
of the mighty mountain Taygetos
Leda lay in love with the Son of Kronos
shrouded in his dark clouds,
and there she gave birth
to children who are saviours.

They save human beings upon the earth
and on their speeding ships
when winter storm winds race
across a ruthless sea.

Then from their ships the seamen cry out,
10 calling for the Sons of Great Zeus,
and they go up to the edge of the stern
and offer them white lambs.

A strong wind and the sea waves
start sinking their ship
beneath the water
when, suddenly,

they appear,
darting through the air
on dusky wings,

and instantly they hold back
the blasts of the cruel winds
and they smooth the waves   15
on the surface of the white sea.

For sailors they are the good signs,
the end of suffering.
When they see them they are glad
and rest from pain and labour.

Farewell, Tyndaridai,
riders of swift horses.
And now I shall remember you
and another song too.

Notes

I HYMN TO DIONYSOS

Dionysos was god of wine, intoxication and ecstasy, son of Zeus and Semele. Semele, at the instigation of Zeus' wife, Hera, had asked Zeus to appear to her as he truly was. When he came to her as lord of lightning, storm and thunderbolt, she was burnt to ashes. The baby was snatched prematurely from his mother's flaming womb and sewn into Zeus' thigh to be born in due time. Hence he is called 'twice-born'. The child was later given to Hermes, who gave him into the care of the nymphs. See hymn XXVI.

Only fragments survive of this hymn, including a section from near the opening, and the closing verses, which are preserved only in the Moscow manuscript of the hymns, rediscovered in 1777 (see Introduction, p. xxviii). The hymn was probably about 400 lines long. The main part may have told the story of how Dionysos rescued Hera, when she had been trapped by her son Hephaistos in a throne from which she could not escape. Dionysos made Hephaistos drunk, and persuaded him to release her. Hera rewarded Dionysos by persuading the other gods to admit him to their company on Olympos. Some verses about this story survive in a papyrus from a poem on this subject, which could possibly be this Homeric hymn. Lines 10–13 are also preserved in another recently published papyrus fragment. Cf. M. L. West, *Zeitschrift für Papyrologie und Epigraphik* 134 (2001), 1–11.

1. *Drakanon*: It is not sure which locality of this name is referred to, but possibly it is a place on the island of Kos.
1–2. *Ikaros, Naxos*: Islands in the Aegean. Naxos was specially sacred to Dionysos.
2. *bull-god*: Dionysos sometimes took the form of a bull. The exact sense of the Greek word (*eiraphiota*) is uncertain.
3. *Alpheios*: A river in the north-west Peloponnese, near Olympia.

4. *Semele*: Daughter of Kadmos and Harmonia, and mother of Dionysos. Dionysos later reclaimed his mother from the Underworld and took her to Olympos, where she became immortal.

Zeus: King of the gods, often called simply the 'Son of Kronos'. Youngest son of the Titans Rhea and Kronos. His epithets, 'cloud-gathering' and 'high-thundering', point to his origins as a weather god of rain and storm, whose weapon was the thunderbolt, while the etymology of his name points to his origins as the Sky Father of the Indo-European peoples.

7. *white-armed Hera*: Sister and wife to Zeus, daughter of the Titans Rhea and Kronos. Her other epithet is 'cow-eyed'. Together Zeus and Hera had three children: Ares, god of war, Eileithyia, goddess of childbirth, and Hebe, goddess of youth. Hera's Roman name was Juno.

8. *Nysa*: A legendary place. It is also the scene of the Rape of Persephone in the 'Hymn to Demeter'.

15. *As these things are three*: We do not know what this refers to. The poet is explaining why Dionysos' festivals are celebrated every third year. The Greeks counted both the first and last in a series, and so this really means once in each alternate year (one, three, five, etc.).

16. *hecatombs*: A hecatomb was originally a sacrifice of a hundred oxen, and then it came to be used of sacrifices more generally.

21. *women-maddening*: Dionysiac possession was seen as a form of madness. Women inspired by the gods were called *maenads* (the Greek word means 'mad women'). See note to hymn II, 386.

25. *Thyone*: Another name for Semele, after her immortalization. It means 'inspired woman', like *maenad* or *bacchant*.

II HYMN TO DEMETER

1. *Demeter*: Daughter of the Titans Kronos and Rhea, and sister of Zeus, Hades and Poseidon, Hestia and Hera. She is the goddess of fertility and the gifts of the earth, especially grain.

2. *her daughter*: Persephone, whose father was Zeus. She was also known simply as Kore, which means 'daughter' or 'girl'.

Aidoneus: Hades, god of the Underworld, brother of Zeus and Poseidon. Their father was Kronos and their mother was Rhea.

5. *Okeanos*: The eldest of the Titans, son of Gaia (Earth) and Ouranos (Heaven). God of the river which encircled the circumference of the earth, in Greek cosmology. He married Tethys, his sister, and they had three thousand sons, who are the earth's rivers, and three thousand daughters, called the Oceanids, nymphs of springs, waters and land, some of whom play with Persephone in the meadow (cf. Hesiod, *Theogony* 337–70).

9. *Gaia*: Goddess of Earth. In Hesiod's *Theogony*, Gaia was the first to arise from Chaos (116–19). Gaia assists Zeus in his plan rather than helping Demeter, suggesting the inherent lawfulness of Persephone's marriage to Hades.

the God Who Receives So Many: Hades.

25. *Hekate*: In Hesiod's *Theogony* (409–52) daughter of Persaios (or Perses) and Asteria, and first cousin of Apollo and Artemis. For Hesiod she is a benevolent goddess with wide-ranging powers. Later she was especially a goddess of the Underworld and of magic, and was worshipped at crossroads.

26. *Helios*: The Sun-god, son of Hyperion and Theia or Euryphaessa, and brother of Selene (Moon) and Eos (Dawn). See hymn XXXI.

47. *Deo*: Demeter.

60. *Rhea*: Daughter of Gaia (Earth) and Ouranos (Heaven). Married her brother Kronos and became mother of six children, Demeter, Zeus, Hades, Poseidon, Hera and Hestia.

92. *Olympos*: The highest mountain in Greece, near the borders of Thessaly and Macedonia, believed to be the home of the gods and ruled by Zeus.

97. *Eleusis*: A settlement on the way from Athens to Megara.

102. *Aphrodite*: Goddess of love. Aphrodite's 'gifts' are love, beauty, fertility, love of life. See hymn V, 1.

105. *Eleusinides*: Son, or descendant, of Eleusinus, the hero after whom Eleusis was named.

120–21. *For it is not wrong to tell the truth*: Demeter actually tells a false tale, similar to ones told by Odysseus in the *Odyssey*, when he claims to be a Cretan.

126. *Thorikos*: A settlement on the north-east coast of Attika.

153. *Triptolemos*: In later Athenian legend he is taught the arts of agriculture by Demeter, and is often shown in art, being given the gift of corn by Demeter.

Dioklos: A hero also celebrated at Megara.

154. *Eumolpos*: The legendary ancestor of the Eumolpidai, the family from whom the Hierophant, or chief priest, of Eleusis was taken. His name means 'Good Singer'. The Hierophant's title means that he 'revealed the sacred things', in the Eleusinian Mysteries.

188–211. *But the goddess stepped on the threshold . . . for the sake of the rite*: The whole of this scene is the model for a series of rituals associated with the Mysteries. Demeter sits on a stool covered in a fleece, with her head veiled. This was re-enacted in a purification ceremony, which formed a preliminary rite before initiation. Initiates also fasted, as Demeter had done, and broke their fast by drinking a special mixture (called a *kykeon*). Iambe's jesting can be linked with various forms of ritual abuse and jesting (some of it obscene) which took place at festivals of Demeter. The hymn implies that drinking the *kykeon* was associated with jesting of this kind.

195. *Iambe*: Her name was invented as an origin for the iambic rhythm, which was originally used especially for satirical and abusive poetry. Later, it became the chief metre used in drama (tragedy and comedy), and was eventually taken over by classicizing English poets in the sixteenth century.

228. *witchcraft*: This may refer to 'attacks' of pain or fever which were ascribed to some demonic agency.

the Undercutter: This must refer to cutting the roots of herbs for magic purposes, to harm someone.

229. *the Woodcutter*: Again refers to someone who cuts magic herbs.

231. *As she said this, she took the child to her fragrant breast*: Demeter's nursing of Demophoon seems to be associated with a theme which is often mentioned in connection with the Mysteries, that of a child born to, or nursed by, the goddess of fertility. The initiates also might see themselves as the adopted children of Demeter, and thus as guaranteed her special favour.

237. *ambrosia*: The divine substance which conveyed immortality.

239. *she buried him in the heart of the fire*: Fire was also seen as a means of achieving immortality, since it burnt away one's mortal elements.

259. *Styx*: One of the daughters of Okeanos, and the name of a river in Arcadia, whose water was thought to emanate from the Underworld. The name means 'shuddering', and Styx was so awe-inspiring that she was regarded with dread even by the gods. Hence she was invoked by them in their oaths.

265. *But in due season ... forever*: Demeter declares the institution of an annual festival in honour of Demophoon, which involved a ritual mock-battle, known as the *Ballētus*, i.e. probably stone-throwing.

272. *Kallichoron*: A well in the sanctuary at Eleusis, whose name means 'of the lovely dancing'. It was the place where sacred dances were celebrated.

314. *Iris*: Messenger of the gods and goddess of the rainbow.

335. *Erebos*: The Underworld ('land of darkness').

336. *Slayer of Argos*: Hermes, the god who acted as messenger to the Underworld. The traditional explanation of his epithet Slayer of Argos was that he had killed the monster Argos who had been appointed by

Hera to watch over Io, when she had been transformed into a cow by Zeus.

372. *gave her to eat a seed of the pomegranate*: Because Persephone ate food given her by Hades, this meant that she must return to him. The pomegranate, symbol of fertility and marriage, but also of blood and death, was often portrayed in art as an attribute of Persephone and Hades.

386. *maenad*: Literally 'mad woman'. The maenads were followers of Dionysos, who celebrated the rites of the god with dancing, leaping and song, wreathed with ivy and 'maddened' with ecstasy. See hymn XXVI.

387–404. *from the other side*: From here to 'Receiver of Many' (404) the manuscript is torn, and parts of verses are missing, but the general sense can be reconstructed with some certainty.

399. *for a third part of the seasons of the year*: Persephone's time with Hades represents the season of winter, when plants and flowers die and there is no new growth.

408. *Ouranos*: The god of Heaven, and father of Kronos and the other Titans.

417–25. *We were all playing in a lovely meadow*: Persephone here names her companions, the daughters of Okeanos. But the list ends with Pallas (Athena) and Artemis, who were not mentioned at the beginning of the hymn. These two goddesses appear in later versions of the Rape, from the fifth century BC onwards.

424. *Pallas*: See hymn XXVIII.

Artemis: See hymns IX and XXVII, and note to hymn III, 15.

450. *the plain of Rarion*: This lay close to the sanctuary of Eleusis, and was later said to have been the place where crops were first grown.

462–79. *whatever you wish*: Again there is a tear here in the manuscript, down to 'stops the voice' (479), but the sense is more or less clear.

478–9. *sacred mysteries . . . stops the voice*: The Eleusinian Mysteries were extremely solemn and secret, and anyone who revealed them, or profaned them in any way, could be liable to punishment by death.

480–82. *Blessed is the one . . . gloom and darkness below*: This proclamation of the special blessings offered by initiation into the Mysteries of Eleusis is echoed by later Greek and Roman writers. Cf., for example, Pindar, 'Blessed is he who has seen these things and goes below the earth: he knows the end of life, he knows the god-given beginning', and Sophocles, 'thrice blessed are those mortals who have seen these rites and enter Hades: for them alone there is life, for the others all things are evil'.

489. *Ploutos*: God of wealth, the gift of the deities of the earth. In Hesiod's *Theogony* he is the son of Demeter and a Cretan man named Iasios. Plouton, the god of the Underworld, is a variant form of the same name.

491. *Paros*: An island in the Cyclades, which had an important cult of Demeter and Persephone.

Antron: A place in Thessaly, near which was a sanctuary of Demeter.

III HYMN TO APOLLO

DELIAN APOLLO

Some modern scholars have argued that lines 1–178 were originally a separate poem, which was later extended with the addition of 179–546, to form the hymn as it is transmitted in our manuscripts. On this question, see Introduction, p. xiii.

1. *Apollo the Archer*: Son of Leto and Zeus, god of prophecy, divination and healing, and of flocks and herds. He was leader of the Muses and lord of music and the arts. As the Archer God, Lord of the Silver Bow, his arrows could bring plague and death.

5. *Leto*: Daughter of the Titans Koios and Phoebe (Hesiod, *Theogony* 404–10) and mother of Apollo and Artemis.

10. *nectar*: The drink of the gods.

15. *Artemis who delights in arrows*: Daughter of Zeus and Leto, twin-sister of Apollo. Virgin huntress, goddess of the wild, and guardian of unmarried girls, women in childbirth, children and young animals. Aeschylus describes her as 'kind to the playful cubs of fierce lions, delighting in the suckling young of every wild creature who roams the fields' (*Agamemnon* 140–43). She was later identified with the moon. The Romans called her Diana.

16. *Ortygia*: 'Quail-island.' Probably an island near Delos (perhaps Rhenaia), although later other places claimed this name.

Delos: A small island in the Aegean, at the centre of the Cyclades.

17. *Kynthian hill*: Kynthos is a hill, 368 feet high, on Delos.

18. *Inopos*: The only stream on Delos.

20. *Phoebus*: A title of Apollo, meaning 'shining' or 'radiant'.

30–46. *The people of Crete . . . make a home for her son*: This passage charts the places visited by Leto in her search for a birthplace for Apollo. All are cities, islands and mountains around and in the Aegean.

62. *Koios*: One of the Titans.

93. *Dione*: Titan goddess, daughter of Gaia (Earth) and Ouranos (Heaven). In Homer, she is a consort of Zeus and mother of Aphrodite (*Iliad* 5.370–417), in contrast to Hesiod's version of Aphrodite's parentage and birth from the sea foam in his *Theogony* (353). Dione's name may be a feminine counterpart of Zeus.

94. *Rhea*: See note to hymn II, 60.

Ichnaean Themis: Titan goddess of Right, daughter of Gaia (Earth) and Ouranos (Heaven), mother of the Horai (Hours, Seasons) and the Fates. In the 'Hymn to the Son of Kronos, Most High', XXIII, Themis sits beside Zeus as the lawfulness of his rule, and in hymn VIII, 4, Ares, god of war, is invoked as her ally, the ally of Law.

Amphitrite: Sea-goddess, wife of Poseidon, daughter of Nereus and Doris, and therefore one of the Nereids.

96. *Eileithyia*: Goddess of childbirth, later associated with Artemis. Homer talks of Eileithyiai in the plural, making them daughters of Hera (*Iliad* 11.269–72; 16. 187–8; 19.95–133). In Hesiod, Eileithyia is the daughter of Zeus and Hera, sister of Hebe and Ares (*Theogony* 921–3).

102. *Iris*: Goddess of the rainbow, messenger of the gods, as in the 'Hymn to Demeter' (II, 314).

147. *Ionians*: Greeks who migrated at the end of the Bronze Age to the central part of the west coast of Asia Minor and the Cyclades. Their dialect was also spoken in Euboea and Attica.

157. *the girls of Delos*: A choir of Delian girls. In later periods the Delian choir continued to be famous, and they were often mentioned in connection with dedications, made by visiting delegations from different parts of the Greek world. Consequently they could well have acquired the skill to imitate different types of speech or dialect, which the poet ascribes to them here.

172. *The blind man who lives in rocky Chios*: Later tradition usually regarded Homer as the author of this hymn. He was believed to have been blind, and to have lived in the island of Chios. The Homeridae, a guild of singers originally claiming descent from Homer, were also based in Chios (see Introduction, p. xiii).

PYTHIAN APOLLO

This, the second part of the 'Hymn to Apollo', is clearly designed as a continuation of the first part, since it contains many passages and motifs which echo ones in the Delian section. It describes Apollo's search for a site for his first and most important oracle, and his choice of Pytho (Delphi) for this.

179. *Lykia*: An area in south-west Asia Minor.

Meonia: Later identified with Lydia, in western Asia Minor.

180. *Miletos*: An important Ionian city on the west coast of Asia Minor.

183. *Pytho*: Delphi is always called Pytho in the Homeric poems and in this hymn.

189. *the Muses*: The nine daughters of Zeus and Mnemosyne, goddess of memory, the inspiration of poets. Apollo was their leader, in songs and dances at the feasts of the gods on Olympos where they lived.

194. *Then the lovely-haired Graces and the kind-hearted Hours*: Trinities of maiden goddesses. In Hesiod's *Theogony* the seasons (Horai) are the three daughters of Zeus and Themis, embodying the lawfulness of nature through the change of seasons and the growth of vegetation, and the Graces (Charites) are daughters of Zeus and Eurunome (901–3, 907–11).

195. *Harmonia*: Daughter of Ares and Aphrodite, given by Zeus to be the wife of Kadmos, legendary founder of Thebes, and mother of Semele, Dionysos' mother.

Hebe: Goddess of youth, daughter of Zeus and Hera, cupbearer to the gods (*Iliad* 4.2), and wife of Herakles in hymn XV (and *Odyssey* 11.603).

200. *Ares*: God of war, son of Zeus and Hera. See hymn VIII.

209. *How you went courting*: This passage seems to be a list of Apollo's amours, but the details are unclear.

the daughter of Azan: Apollo and Ischys were rival suitors of Koronis, who became the mother of Asklepios by Apollo. (The correct text is not certain here.)

211. *Phorbas*: It is not clear whether Phorbas is another rival of Apollo. Later the name is sometimes given to a brigand killed by Apollo, and sometimes to a boy loved by him.

Ereutheus: He is unknown and again the reading is not certain here.

212. *Leukippos*: This is probably the son of Perieres, who shared a claim with Apollo to be father of Phoebe and Hilaeira. Possibly there was a race between the two suitors, with Apollo running and Leukippos in a chariot.

216–93. *First you went to Pieria*: This is the beginning of a long description of places visited by Apollo in northern Greece, on his way to the site of Delphi. This geographical catalogue complements the one in the Delian section, about Leto's quest for a birthplace.

Pieria is just north of Mount Olympos. Apollo then travels south through Thessaly and crosses to Euboea. From here he crosses the strait between Euboea and the mainland (Euripos) and goes west through Boeotia (including the site of Thebes, still unoccupied).

At Onchestos, south of Lake Kopais, the poet pauses to describe a special custom at Poseidon's sanctuary. At Telphousa, further west, Apollo is dissuaded by the nymph of the spring from building his temple there. Finally he reaches Krisa, on the north side of the Gulf of Corinth and decides to found his sanctuary here.

230. *Onchestos, Poseidon's shining grove*: The poet pays a special tribute to Apollo's uncle, Poseidon (the brother of Zeus and Hades), who had a cult at Onchestos. In the 'Hymn to Poseidon' (XXII, 5) he is called a tamer of horses. It is not clear what is the custom or ritual which is being described here. The sanctuary was on the top of a ridge, beside a road, and it looks as if the drivers of chariots drawn by young colts were expected to go through the sacred grove on foot, giving their horses respite. If a chariot were broken as they passed through it became the god's property.

This is a possible interpretation, but there is no consensus about whether it is right, or exactly why this should have been done.

244. *Telphousa*: Later Apollo returns and sets up a cult here, at the spring of Telphousa. A later tradition also made this the place where the prophet Teiresias died and was buried. This suggests that the cult and spring were associated with prophecy.

251. *Europe*: In early Greek literature this refers to northern and central Greece, as opposed to the Peloponnese.

269. *Krisa beneath the cleft of Parnassos*: The actual site of Krisa was probably on a rocky spur above the Pleistos river valley, below Delphi. Here it is used of the general area in which the sanctuary was to be founded, and later it is also applied to the harbour where Apollo lands with his priests.

275–6. *so that she alone . . . Far-Shooter*: Telphousa does not want to share her honours with the god.

278. *Phlegyes*: In later tradition they were brigands who attacked travellers to Delphi, or Delphi itself, until they were wiped out by Apollo.

283–5. *where the shoulder . . . underneath*: This vivid passage has been taken as a description of the site of Krisa, but it seems more likely that it refers to the actual site of Delphi.

296–7. *The sons of Erginos, Trophonios and Agamedes*: They were legendary master-builders, rewarded for their piety with an early death. Trophonios was the hero of an important oracular cult at Lebadeia in Boeotia.

296. *the threshold of well-based stones*: The threshold of Apollo's Delphic temple is also mentioned in the *Iliad* (9.404–5) and *Odyssey* (8.79–81), and must therefore have already been an important feature.

298. *And the numberless tribes . . . around the temple*: The order of verses is not certain here, but if this reading is correct it could refer to the league of communities which were around Delphi and who later administered the sanctuary, the so-called Amphictionic League.

300–302. *the great fat she-dragon*: Apollo's killing of the serpent or dragon of Delphi (later called Python) was a major exploit, commemorated in the cult there.

305–6. *Once she received . . . Typhaon*: Into the story of the killing of the Delphic dragon is inserted the parallel myth of Typhaon (also called Typhon or Typhoeus), who is here described as the offspring of Hera. In Hesiod's *Theogony* (820–80) this monster is the child of Earth and Tartaros, and the last great enemy of Zeus who has to be defeated before Zeus can become ruler of the world.

308–9. *because the Son of Kronos had given birth himself . . . from his head*: Zeus was Athena's sole parent, and she was born, fully armed, from his head. This is described in hymn XXVIII.

317. *my son Hephaistos*: In Homer he is the son of Zeus and Hera, although Hesiod makes him a child of Hera alone, produced in revenge at Athena's birth from Zeus (*Theogony* 924–9). The story of how he was thrown from heaven and rescued by Thetis is also mentioned in the *Iliad* (18.394–405).

335. *Titan gods*: The Titans were the older generation of gods, children of Earth and Heaven. They fought against Zeus and the other gods of his generation, and were punished by being confined to Tartaros, at the lowest level of the universe.

358–62. *Then, heavily, she lay there . . . breathing out blood*: This passage describing the serpent's death throes had its counterpart in a vivid and detailed musical representation of the event, played on the flute at the Pythian Games. These games were supposed originally to have been instituted by Apollo to commemorate his victory. The first recorded victor in the flute-playing contest, however, was Sacadas in 586 BC

363. *Now you rot right here*: The Greek word meaning 'to rot' (*pūthein*) is made the origin of the name Pytho (*Pūtho*) for the place of Apollo's worship, and Apollo's title *Pūthios*.

368. *Chimaira*: Daughter of Typhaon and Echidna, killed by Bellerophon. She had three heads, of a lion, goat and snake. Cf. Hesiod, *Theogony* 319–25.

369. *Hyperion*: Literally 'He who travels above', the Titan father of the Sun-god Helios, but used here interchangeably with Helios (371, below). Son of Gaia (Earth) and Ouranos (Heaven), and married to Theia, or Euruphaessa (hymn XXXI).

375. *Then Phoebus Apollo understood in his mind*: This may imply that Telphousa deliberately sent Apollo to Delphi in order that he should become a victim of the dragon.

386. *calling him Telphousian*: The story thus accounts for another of Apollo's cult-titles, Telphousios. There was a variant spelling, Delphousios, which would have suggested a link with Delphi.

388. *Then Phoebus Apollo wondered in his heart*: This introduces the theme of the last section of the hymn, Apollo's choice of his first priests.

393. *Cretans from Knossos, the city of Minos*: Minos was the legendary ruler of Knossos, from whose name is derived the modern term 'Minoan', which is used to denote the civilization of Crete in the late Bronze Age. The cult of Apollo was important in Crete in historical times, and this tradition about the Cretan origin of his Delphic ministers may represent a real link between Crete and Delphi at the beginning of its history as a place of cult.

398. *sandy Pylos*: A settlement on the west coast of the Peloponnese. Pylos is the home of King Nestor in Homer, and a late Bronze Age palace has been excavated in the south-west of the Peloponnese, which is thought to be Nestor's Pylos.

409. *First they passed by Maleia*: Here begins the third and final geographical catalogue of this hymn, which describes the ship's course as the wind takes it westwards round the Peloponnese and then into the Gulf of Corinth, until it reaches Krisa. These three catalogues together cover a large part of the Greek world (the Aegean Sea, northern and southern Greece), suggesting the universality of Apollo's power. Maleia is a cape at the south-east end of the Peloponnese.

410. *the Lakonian coast*: South of Sparta.

412. *Tainaron*: A settlement at the end of the central cape of the Peloponnese.

421–2. *So sailing on its course the ship reached Arene*: In this passage various places on the west coast of the Peloponnese are listed. Pylos is here located on the north-west coast (as already in some passages in the *Iliad*), further north than the site of the Bronze Age palace.

428–9. *the steep mountain of Ithaka . . . Zakynthos*: The group of Ionian islands off the west coast of Greece.

431. *the boundless gulf of Krisa*: i.e. the Gulf of Corinth.

443. *He entered his shrine through the precious tripods*: The poet speaks as though Apollo's sanctuary already exists. Bronze tripods (cauldrons on feet) were valuable commodities which were dedicated to the gods in early Greek times, and there were said to be some standing in or in front of Apollo's temple at Delphi.

495. *pray to me as Delphinios*: Apollo's transformation into a dolphin

here accounts for a third cult-title, Delphinios, which was common throughout Greece.

500. *singing the Paean in praise of the Healer*: The *paean* was a lyric song in honour of Apollo (or sometimes other gods), often sung in thanksgiving for victory, or deliverance from some threat such as disease, etc. The refrain *iēēpaiēon* was also used as a title of the god himself.

540–542. *But if, in word or deed, ... by force forever*: Apollo warns them that if they act unjustly they will lose their freedom and control of his cult. In the 590s BC the people of Krisa were accused of acting in an extortionate way towards Delphic pilgrims, and after a war involving a number of Greek states (the 'First Sacred War') Krisa was destroyed. In later times Delphi was administered by the so-called Amphictionic League. Some scholars believe that Apollo's prophecy refers to this series of events, but this is not universally accepted.

IV HYMN TO HERMES

1. *Hermes*: The trickster god of deception, son of Zeus and Maia, messenger of the gods. His range extends from simple thieving and bartering to being the one who invents the lyre, the shepherd's pipes, and the art of making fire, and he becomes the guardian of flocks and their fertility. As the only god who can cross the boundary between the living and the dead, he is called Psychopompos, the guide of souls (see note to l. 572). He is the god who brings luck to mortals: a *hermaion* was a lucky find, a windfall. The hymn charts his theft of Apollo's cattle as a means of trading with Apollo in order to win a place on Olympos for himself and his mother. The Romans called him Mercury.

Maia: Daughter of the Titan Atlas and Pleione, and later identified as one of the seven Pleiades. Her name means 'mother' or 'nurse'.

2. *Kyllene*: A mountain in Arcadia, second highest in the Peloponnese (7,800 feet).

3. *who brings luck*: The sense of the Greek word (*eriounios*) is uncertain, and this is only one ancient interpretation. Modern scholarship favours the sense 'fast runner'.

51. *seven harmonious strings of sheep-gut*: The seven-stringed lyre is first mentioned here in Greek literature. Its invention was attributed to the poet Terpander (mid-seventh century BC), although it appears already in late Bronze Age art.

55–6. *The god then, improvising ... taunt each other*: This seems to refer to the practice of improvisation of comic or abusive songs, sung alternately as a form of contest at feasts or symposia.

73. *sharp-eyed Slayer of Argos*: See note to hymn II, 336.

99. *Selene*: The goddess of the moon. Selene is here the daughter of the Titan Pallas, son of Megamedes. Megamedes does not occur elsewhere. In Hesiod's *Theogony* (371-4) she is a daughter of Hyperion and Theia, in hymn XXXI of Hyperion and Euryphaessa.

109. *and trimmed it with a knife*: It is possible that one or two lines have been lost here, describing the process of making fire. Hermes sharpens a stick and uses it like a drill, to start a fire by using friction.

125-6. *and even now, ... without end*: Either the skins were on show as relics, or a rock formation was said to represent them.

128. *twelve portions*: Presumably for twelve Olympian gods. There was a cult of the Twelve Gods at Olympia, near the river Alpheios, so this ritual may be giving the origin of this. The names of the twelve varied in different parts of Greece, but Hermes himself was usually included. Hermes, however, does not eat any of the meat here, either because he is sacrificing on behalf of the other gods, or perhaps because in Greek sacrifices the gods received the smoke from the fat which was roasted, and the meat was usually eaten by men.

183. *Zeus who holds the aegis*: The aegis was a supernatural weapon of Zeus, similar to a shield, which was also used by Athena and Apollo. It struck terror into opponents of the gods, and could also create storms when shaken.

184. *Dawn*: Eos, goddess of dawn, sister of Helios and Selene. See hymn XXXI, where she is given 'arms of rose'. Homer calls her 'rosy-fingered' (*Odyssey* 5.121).

213. *He saw a bird*: Birds were ominous for the Greeks: they were sources of information about the gods. It is ironic that Apollo, himself god of divination (and often considered omniscient), should need assistance from a human witness, or a bird.

216. *holy Pylos*: As in the 'Hymn to Apollo', Pylos must be located near the river Alpheios.

219. *this fantastic thing*: It is an essential part of Hermes' strategy to confuse Apollo's clear thinking, and even to show it to be comic.

224. *a centaur*: A hybrid creature of Greek mythology, with human head and equine body.

259. *the leader of the little people*: The little people must mean the souls of the dead. The word for 'little' (*oligos*) may possibly mean 'weak' here. In the end Hermes actually does become the god responsible for leading ghosts down to Hades (Psychopompos), as in book 24 of the *Odyssey*.

295. *he let off an omen*: Hermes breaks wind, and then sneezes. Such sudden, semi-voluntary physical events could be treated as omens!

379. *I didn't drive his cows home*: Hermes is strictly speaking telling the truth, as he left the cows by the Alpheios, and slipped into his cave by the keyhole!

381. *Helios I honour greatly*: The all-seeing Sun-god was the supreme witness of right and wrong.

383. *But I will swear a great oath*: As god of deception Hermes is also master of the art of swearing oaths, i.e. denying a crime without perjuring oneself.

415–16. *intent on hiding his purpose, his eyes flashing fire*: The text and interpretation are uncertain here.

429–30. *Mnemosyne*: Goddess of memory, daughter of Gaia (Earth) and Ouranos (Heaven). She lay nine nights with Zeus and gave birth to the nine Muses (see Hesiod, *Theogony* 52–63). Hermes belonged to her by virtue of his skill in music.

460. *shaft of cornel wood*: Apollo swears by the cornel-wood staff (or spear) which he is carrying, just as Achilles swears by the sceptre he holds (*Iliad* 1.234–9).

473. *And so now ... these things*: The text is corrupt, but this sense seems probable.

527–8. *I shall make you a perfect symbol ... in my heart*: Text and interpretation are uncertain here. A *sumbolon* was originally a 'tally', i.e. one of two halves or corresponding pieces of an object which two contracting parties broke between them, each keeping one half. So it comes to mean a token, guarantee, contract or symbol.

529. *a marvellous wand*: The wand (*Greek kerukeion*, Latin *caduceus*) of Hermes, which seems to have combined the functions of a herald's sceptre, shepherd's staff and magic wand.

552–4. *There are certain holy ones, sisters born*: Apollo gives Hermes a form of prophecy which he learnt as a boy, separate from the inspiration of his father Zeus. This derives from three 'holy maidens' who live under Parnassos, and who seem to take the form of bees, which were considered divine or prophetic creatures.

Other sources speak of three nymphs of Parnassos called Thriae, who were nurses of Apollo and who invented a form of divination with pebbles (used in drawing lots, or *cleromancy*).

572. *the only consecrated messenger to Hades*: Hermes as Psychopompos, guide of souls on their journey to and from the Underworld. In the *Odyssey*, he leads the souls of the dead suitors down to Hades, gibbering like bats (24.1–14), and in the 'Hymn to Demeter' he leads Persephone back to her mother from Hades (334–86). He also led the living Orpheus to the Underworld to bring Eurydice back, but Orpheus looked behind him at his wife and she vanished.

V HYMN TO APHRODITE

1. *Aphrodite*: Goddess of love. For her birth, see introductory note to hymn VI. Aphrodite was married to Hephaistos, and was the lover of Ares and various mortal men. With Ares she had three children, Harmonia, Terror and Fear. The Romans knew her as Venus.

2. *Cyprian*: Aphrodite's cult was most prominent in Cyprus, and it was probably from here that it first came to Greece.

6. *Cytherean*: Because she was born in the sea near the island of Cythera, south of the Peloponnese.

7. *But there are three hearts*: The poet pays tribute to three virgin goddesses.

8. *Athena*: Goddess of battle and of crafts. See hymn XXVIII.

16. *Artemis*: Goddess of hunting, dancing and unmarried girls. See notes to hymns III, 15, and XXVII.

22. *Hestia*: Goddess of the hearth, the centrepiece of the home. In Hesiod's *Theogony* she is the first-born child of Kronos, but later when he has swallowed and then disgorged his children she is reborn last (453–4, 493–7). See hymn XXIV.

53. *Anchises*: A Trojan leader, son of Kapys and Themiste, and great-grandson of Tros, eponymous ancestor of the Trojans. The tale of Aphrodite's love for Anchises is also found in the *Iliad* (2.819–21; 5.311–13), and in Hesiod (*Theogony* 1008–10).

54. *Ida*: The main mountain range of the Troad.

59. *Paphos*: Aphrodite's chief sanctuary, in south-west Cyprus.

61. *the Graces*: See note to hymn III, 194.

97. *Nymphs*: Female spirits of nature, very long-lived or immortal, who belong to a particular place: mountain nymphs, water-nymphs, tree-nymphs, sea-nymphs.

111–12. *Otreus*: This may be the Otreus who is king of the Phrygians, together with Mygdon, in the *Iliad* (3.184–6). Phrygia was a country near the Troad in Asia Minor.

177. *son of Dardanos*: Dardanos was an ancestor of Anchises and son of Zeus.

196. *who will rule among the Trojans*: Aphrodite prophesies that Aeneas will take over the kingship, as also foretold in the *Iliad* 20.307–8.

198. *Aeneas shall be his name*: The name (Aineias in Greek) is explained

here as due to the 'terrible grief' (*ainon achos*) of Aphrodite. When the boy grew up he married Creusa, a daughter of King Priam of Troy, and they had a son, Ascanius. In the *Iliad* Aeneas' bravery in defending Troy is second only to that of Hector. He is wounded by Diomedes but is saved by his mother, Aphrodite, and then by Apollo (5.166–453). He also fights with Achilles and is only saved from death when Poseidon transports him to the edge of the field. Poseidon tells the other gods that it is Aeneas' destiny to survive, so that he and his descendants will rule over the Trojans (20.75–350). Virgil's *Aeneid* continues this idea, making Aeneas the founder of the Roman race. The moving image of Aeneas carrying his father Anchises on his back, and leading his son Ascanius by the hand among the ruins of Troy, comes in the *Aeneid*. His wife Creusa follows them, but is lost in the burning city. When Aeneas goes back to find her, he meets only her spirit, who tells him that the gods want him to found a new kingdom in Italy.

202. *Ganymede*: Son of Tros, carried off to heaven because of Zeus' love for him.

218. *Tithonos*: Son of Laomedon and husband of Eos, the goddess of dawn.

262. *Sileni*: Here probably the same as the Satyrs, nature-demons with features of animals (horses or goats), who accompanied Dionysos and pursued the nymphs. Later, Silenos was used especially as the name of their leader.

280. *Ilion*: Troy.

286. *But if you ever mention it*: In later tradition Anchises did boast of his liaison, and was punished with physical incapacity (being maimed or blinded). The poet is probably alluding to this story here.

VI HYMN TO APHRODITE

There are two versions of Aphrodite's birth, one from Homer (see note to hymn III, 93), and one from Hesiod. In Hesiod's tale, Gaia (Earth) and Ouranos (Heaven) brought forth the Titans and other offspring, whom Ouranos hated and hid within Gaia, not letting them see the light. Gaia gave Kronos a sickle, and as Heaven lay stretched out upon Earth, Kronos harvested his father's genitals and threw them into the sea. His genitals settled in the lap of the waves, and from the foam (*aphros*) which gathered about them Aphrodite was born (*Theogony* 154–206). This hymn follows the Hesiodic version.

3. *where Zephyros swept her*: In Hesiod's version the sea carries her near to Cythera, and then to Cyprus, where she sets foot on the land (188–200). Zephyros is the west wind. Botticelli's *Birth of Venus* depicts this scene (see Introduction, p. xxiv).

12. *the gold-filleted Hours*: The Seasons (Horai). See note to hymn III, 194. The Hours, assisted by the Graces, clothe Aphrodite in her temple at Paphos in Cyprus (cf. hymn V, 58–63). This is where she goes, in the song Demodokos sings in the *Odyssey*, after her humiliation by Hephaistos who caught her and Ares in an invisible net and invited the gods to watch them: 'And there the Graces washed her body and anointed her with the ambrosial oil that the immortals use. And when they had clothed her in her lovely garments, she was a wonder to behold' (*Odyssey* 8.362–6).

VII HYMN TO DIONYSOS

The hymn offers yet another instance of the way that the divinity of the gods is imagined as unrecognizable in their relations with human beings. Demeter was mistaken for an old nurse by Metaneira and her girls; Aphrodite was taken for a young girl 'so like a goddess' by Anchises. It takes the wisdom of the helmsman to know a god when he sees one.

8. *Tyrrhenians*: A non-Greek people who occupied some of the islands of the Aegean, and were later identified with the Etruscans.

29. *the Hyperboreans*: A legendary people (living in the far north of the earth). The name means 'beyond the north wind'. Apollo would visit the Hyperboreans every winter. Pindar writes of them as living in an earthly paradise without disease, old age or strife, where they would sing and dance and worship Apollo (*Olympian Ode* 3.11–34; *Pythian Ode* 10.29–46). They were connected with Delos and Delphi, the birthplace and the chief oracular sanctuary of Apollo.

VIII HYMN TO ARES

The style of this hymn is quite different from that of the others, and it is usually thought to have been written in the late Roman period (fourth century AD or later). It has been suggested that it really belongs to the collection of hymns by the Neoplatonist philosopher Proclus, since some of the language resembles these.

Ares, son of Zeus and Hera, was god of war in its most brutal aspect, in contrast to Athena, who presided over the disciplined use of war to protect a community. Ares' sons were Terror (Phobos), and Fear (Deimos) who often came with him to the battlefield, as did Strife (Eris). Zeus says to Ares: 'To me you are the most hateful of all the gods who live on Olympos, for always strife is dear to your heart, and wars, and battles' (cf. *Iliad* 4.440; 5.890–91).

Ares is here identified with his planet: this is in 'the third orbit' (8), because Mars was placed third in the planetary system, counting from the one furthest from earth. Unusually, as god of war he is asked in this hymn to put an end to turmoil in the soul and send it true courage and peace.

4. *father of war-winning Victory*. In Hesiod's *Theogony*, the goddess of victory (Nike) is the daughter of the Oceanid Styx and the Titan Pallas (383–4). With her sister Might (Bia), and her brothers Power (Kratos) and Aspiration (Zelos), she supported Zeus in his battle against the Titans. Ares is here Nike's father in a symbolic sense only.

IX HYMN TO ARTEMIS

3. *Meles*: A river near Smyrna in Asia Minor.
5. *Klaros*: Mentioned in the 'Hymn to Apollo' (40) this was located near the city of Kolophon on the coast of Asia Minor. It had a temple and an oracle dedicated to Apollo.

X HYMN TO APHRODITE

4. *Salamis*: A town on the east coast of Cyprus.

XI HYMN TO ATHENA

For Athena's parentage and birth, see hymn XXVIII.

2. *With Ares*: Athena and Ares are rarely invoked together because of their different attitudes to war. In the *Iliad*, there is a brief contest between them when Ares attacks Athena who responds by striking him to the ground with a blow from a stone and laughs at him (21.391–

433). In hymn V, however, Athena is described as delighting in wars and the work of Ares (10).

XII HYMN TO HERA

Hera, wife of Zeus, was goddess of marriage and childbirth, whose own marriage with Zeus was portrayed as one of strife and reconciliation. In the *Iliad*, for example, she borrows Aphrodite's girdle to render herself irresistible to Zeus in order to distract him from the battlefield and prevent him from assisting the Trojans (14.153–353). Her lame, misshapen son Hephaistos, whom (in one version) she conceived alone, sent her a golden throne with invisible fetters attached to it, in revenge for her act of throwing him out of Olympos for his deformity. Only the wine of Dionysos could induce him to release her (see introductory note to hymn I, and note to III, 317). Her commonest epithets are 'white-armed' and 'cow-eyed'.

XIV HYMN TO THE MOTHER OF THE GODS

This figure is usually identified with Rhea, the mother of various Olympian deities, and Kybele, a goddess of Asia Minor. The instruments mentioned in the hymn were used in her cult, which resembled that of Dionysos, since both involved ecstatic music and dancing of an eastern kind. She was also a goddess of wild animals, and was portrayed accompanied by lions.

XV HYMN TO HERAKLES, THE LION-HEARTED

Herakles was son of Alkmene and Zeus. Hera, angered by Zeus' boast that his son by Alkmene would be the greatest ruler, interfered with the births of Herakles and Eurystheus, delaying Herakles' birth and speeding up Eurystheus' birth, so that Eurystheus became king of Argos instead of Herakles (*Iliad* 19.95–133). So the 'lion-hearted' Herakles had to serve the cruel and cowardly Eurystheus for twelve years, and perform his Labours on behalf of mankind. He was rewarded with immortality, and marriage to Hebe, goddess of youth. Cf. Hesiod, *Theogony*, 950–55.

XVI HYMN TO ASKLEPIOS

Asklepios was son of Apollo and Koronis and became a god of healing. Koronis, already pregnant by Apollo, slept with Ischys, son of Elatos (mentioned in 'Hymn to Apollo', 210). A raven saw her making love with Ischys and flew to Apollo to tell him. Apollo cursed the raven, turning it black, and all ravens have been black ever since. Apollo sent Artemis to kill Koronis, but he snatched her baby from her body as she lay burning on the pyre. He gave Asklepios to the centaur Chiron, who taught him the arts of medicine. Zeus struck Asklepios down with a thunderbolt when he brought someone back from the dead, because in so doing he had transgressed the boundaries of mortality. Cf. Pindar, *Pythian Ode 3*.

His principal sanctuaries were at Epidauros and on the island of Kos. People would come to sleep in his sanctuaries and dream of the god, who healed them, appearing in the form of a man or a snake. He is usually pictured leaning on his staff, with his snake coiled around it. The Romans called him Aesculapius.

3. *the fields of Dotion*: A plain in Thessaly.

XVII HYMN TO THE DIOSKOUROI

Kastor and Polydeukes (Latin Castor and Pollux) were the twin sons of Leda and Zeus, and brothers of Helen and Klytemnestra. They were called Tyndaridai because Leda was married to Tyndareus. In some versions Kastor and Klytemnestra were children of Tyndareus, and Polydeukes and Helen of Zeus. Hence, after Kastor's death, the twins are allowed to share immortality on alternate days.

3. *Mount Taygetos*: The mountain on the west side of Lakonia, where they had a special cult.
5. *riders on swift horses*: They were patrons of horsemanship, or sometimes Kastor was the horseman and Polydeukes a boxer.

XVIII HYMN TO HERMES

4. *Atlas*: A Titan, and father, with the Oceanid Pleione, of the Pleiades and Kalypso. Because of his role in the war of the Titans against Zeus, he was condemned to hold up the sky for ever, and was later identified with the Atlas Mountains in North Africa. He had one brief reprieve, when Herakles came to steal the golden apples from the Hesperides, the daughters of Evening, in the far west of the earth. Herakles offered to hold the sky up for him if he would pick the golden fruit from the garden of the Hesperides. He agreed to do this, planning to leave Herakles in his place. But Herakles outwitted him by asking for a cushion for his head, so the giant took back the sky for a moment, which lasted for eternity. In the sixteenth century the image of Atlas with the world on his back inspired the geographer Mercator to call his book of maps an 'atlas'. In modern architecture Atlantes are columns in the form of male figures, used to support an entablature. Cf. *Odyssey* 1.51–4; Hesiod, *Theogony* 507–20; Aeschylus, *Prometheus Bound* 347–50, 425–30; Apollodorus, *Library* 2.5.11.

XIX HYMN TO PAN

Pan was the god of shepherds and flocks, and of the wildest, most inaccessible regions of nature. Born in Arcadia, in this hymn he is a son of Hermes and the daughter of Dryops, called Dryope, who was probably a wood nymph. He was part-goat, part-man and would wander through the uninhabited places of the earth, pursuing nymphs and playing his reed pipes which he had invented himself. He was a god of fertility and hunting, and his worshippers would beat his statue with sea-squills to enliven his powers.

16–18. *not even she . . . song*: The nightingale.
21. *Echo*: A nymph of Mount Helikon. In later legend Pan desired Echo who continually rejected him. She herself fell in love with Narcissus, who in turn rejected her. She pined away, leaving behind only her voice.
47. *They called him Pan . . . all*: The Greek word *pās* (neuter *pān*) means 'all'. His name is also the origin of 'panic', an irrational fear which can possess groups of people or animals.

XX HYMN TO HEPHAISTOS

The crippled god of fire and hence (like Athena) of crafts. He was the
god of metal-working, and made fine jewellery, a golden throne for his
mother Hera (see hymn XII), and palaces for the gods in bronze, with
wheels and tripods of gold. He is shown in the *Iliad* working at his
forge and anvil, a sweating, panting figure of huge bulk, with a shaggy
chest, slender legs and nimble feet. He fashioned the armour for
Achilles, at Thetis' request, including his intricately decorated shield
in silver and gold, tin and bronze (18.368–617). Hephaistos made
Pandora out of the raw material of earth – 'the price for the blessing
of fire' – while Athena clothed and veiled her and set upon her head a
wreath of blossoms, together with a golden crown which Hephaistos
had made for her (Hesiod, *Theogony* 570–89).

Hephaistos (Latinized spelling, Hephaestus) was known as Vulcan
by the Romans.

XXI HYMN TO APOLLO

3. *Peneios*: River in Thessaly which flows into the sea south of Mount
Olympos.
4. *At the beginning and at the end it is always of you*: Apollo was the
leader of the Muses, and in hymn III at his birth he declares that the
lyre and the curved bow belong to him. Hesiod describes himself as
being taught by the Muses to sing, and ordered to praise them at the
beginning and end of his song (*Theogony* 21–34). See also hymns III,
186–206, and XXV.

XXII HYMN TO POSEIDON

Poseidon: God of the sea and also of earthquakes, hence 'Shaker of the
Earth', son of Rhea and Kronos, brother to Zeus and Hades, Hera,
Demeter and Hestia.

3. *Helikon and broad Aigai*: Poseidon had cults at Helike and Aigion,
on the north coast of the Peloponnese, but it is uncertain whether these
are the same places or elsewhere.

XXIII HYMN TO THE SON OF
KRONOS, MOST HIGH

Zeus, king of the gods, is here portrayed in the role of wise law-giver, as the presence of Themis indicates. In Hesiod's *Theogony* (901–6), Themis is called Zeus' second wife. Her daughters, the Horai (Seasons), are Eunomia (Good Law), Dike (Justice) and Eirene (Peace), suggesting how for the Greeks human law came from divine or natural law. She was also mother to the three Fates, Klotho, Atropos and Lachesis, who order the beginning and end of life and the quality of life in between. See also note to hymn III, 94.

XXIV HYMN TO HESTIA

1. *Hestia*: Goddess of the hearth and its sacred fire, worshipped in every household and civic community. Impervious to the arts of Aphrodite (hymn V, 21–32), she refused the attentions of Poseidon and Apollo and swore an oath of chastity, for which Zeus rewarded her with the guardianship of the hearth. She was known to the Romans as Vesta.

the house of the archer Lord Apollo: The sacred hearth at Delphi was regarded as the central point of the world.

3. *soft oil*: It was the custom to pour sacrificial oil on the heads of statues of the gods and goddesses.

XXV HYMN TO THE MUSES AND APOLLO

Lines 1–6 of this hymn are imitations of parts of Hesiod's hymn to the Muses, at the opening of his *Theogony* (1, 94–7, 104). In the *Theogony* the statement that 'kings come from Zeus' is more relevant, since Hesiod has been talking about how both singers and rulers may be divinely inspired.

XXVI HYMN TO DIONYSOS

1. *Ivy-haired loud-roaring Dionysos*: Ivy was sacred to this god, and his cult-title Bromios means 'roaring', probably because of the noise of the instruments used in his worship.

XXVII HYMN TO ARTEMIS

Artemis, like her brother Apollo, is rendered here with all the ambivalence of a goddess of the wild: ferocious huntress with her golden arrows, yet, once her curved bow is hung up, gracefully leading the dances with the Muses and Charites.

XXVIII HYMN TO ATHENA

Athena was the daughter of Metis and Zeus. Metis, daughter of Okeanos and Tethys, became Zeus' first wife, and while she was pregnant with her daughter Zeus learned from his grandmother, Gaia, that if a son were born to her he would lose his power. So he swallowed Metis whole to prevent the birth of the second child, and so that the goddess could counsel him. When it was time for Athena to be born, Hephaistos took his axe and split Zeus' head open, and out sprang Athena fully armed for battle (Hesiod, *Theogony* 886–900, 924–6). *Metis* means intelligence, craft, or counsel. Hence Athena is goddess of wisdom and craft.

2. *with gleaming eyes*: A frequent epithet of Athena, *glaukopis*, referring to a certain depth of vision, pointing to her origins as daughter of Metis. The wise owl was her particular bird, appearing with her on the coinage of Athens, the city that bears her name, to whom she also gave the gift of the olive.

4. *Tritogeneia*: Title of Athena whose meaning is unknown.

13. *The brilliant son of Hyperion*: Helios, the Sun-god.

XXIX HYMN TO HESTIA

4–6. *Without you . . . to Hestia*: At sacrifices she received the first and last libations, being the first- and last-born child of Kronos. See note to hymn V, 22.

7. *And you, too, Slayer of Argos*: Hermes and Hestia were closely associated in cult.

XXX HYMN TO GAIA, MOTHER OF ALL

In Hesiod's *Theogony*, Gaia was the first to arise from Chaos, and in that sense is the oldest deity and the Mother of all that came after (116–200). Next came Tartaros and then Eros (Love), while from Chaos came Night and Erebos. Night united with Erebos to give birth to Day and Aither. Earth's first-born is starry Heaven, and then the hills and nymphs and the sea, Pontos. Only then did she lie with Heaven, and together they brought forth the Titans and various other deities.

6. *It is you who give life to mortals and who take life away*: Aeschylus echoes these words: 'Yea summon Earth, who brings all things to life/ and rears and takes again into her womb' (*The Libation Bearers* 127–8).

XXXI HYMN TO HELIOS

Some scholars have thought that this hymn and its companion, to Selene, were composed later than most of the others, because of their language and style.

Helios, the Sun-god, was known to the Romans as Sol.

From the fifth century BC onwards Apollo was sometimes identified with Helios, and his epithet Phoibos ('shining', Latin Phoebus) could also be applied to the Sun.

2. *Kalliope*: Eldest of the Muses, and inspirer of epic song.
3. *Euryphaessa*: Her name means 'broadly shining', and she is only mentioned here. Hesiod makes Theia the mother of Sun, Moon and Dawn.
6. *Eos*: Goddess of dawn.
8. *he shines down upon all things*: It was Helios to whom Demeter and Hekate went to ask where her daughter had gone, and who could tell them she had been carried off by Hades ('Hymn to Demeter', 22–7, 62–89). He also noticed the love affair of Aphrodite and Ares, informing Aphrodite's husband, Hephaistos, who imprisoned the lovers beneath a snare of gossamer threads hung from the bedposts, as fine as spiders' webs (*Odyssey* 8.270–71). As the one who saw everything, Helios was often called upon to witness oaths. In *Iliad*

3.277, Agamemnon, praying, calls first on Zeus and then on Helios, 'who sees all things and hears all things'.

11. *cheek-pieces*: Helios is clothed as a golden-helmeted chariot-rider, who drives his horses from east to west in the day, bringing light to the world. At night, he was thought to float in a golden bowl from west to east along the river of Ocean which circled the earth. Selene, the Moon, rose from the waters of Ocean at night.

18–19 *the race of beings ... half-divine*: The race of heroes or demigods.

XXXII HYMN TO SELENE

Selene was goddess of the Moon, Luna in Latin. She was later identified with Artemis (Diana).

10. *she speeds them eagerly on, these horses*: Like Helios, Selene also drives a golden chariot drawn by horses, or sometimes oxen.

15. *Pandia*: Originally perhaps an epithet of the full Moon, and also the name of a festival at Athens celebrated on the day of the full moon.

Selene also fell in love with Endymion, the beautiful king of Elis, with whom she had fifty daughters (Pausanias 5.1.3–5). Zeus allowed Endymion to choose his fate, and he chose to sleep for ever and remain for ever young. Selene was said to visit him at night in his cave on Mount Latmos (Apollodorus 1.7.5).

Another lover of Selene was the god Pan, who wooed her clothed in the shining fleece of a white ram, or with the gift of a ram's fleece (Virgil, *Georgics* 3.391–3).

XXXIII HYMN TO THE DIOSKOUROI

See introductory note to hymn XVII.

12. *when, suddenly, they appear*: The Dioskouroi are identified here with the electrical phenomenon called St Elmo's Fire, lights which appear on the masts or sails of ships during storms.

ARISTOPHANES

Lysistrata and Other Plays

*'We women have the salvation of Greece in
our hands'*

Writing at a time of political and social crisis in Athens,
Aristophanes (c. 447–c. 385 BC) was an eloquent, yet bawdy,
challenger to the demagogue and the sophist. In *Lysistrata* and
The Acharnians, two pleas for an end to the long war between
Athens and Sparta, a band of women and a lone peasant respec-
tively defeat the political establishment. The darker comedy of
The Clouds satirizes Athenian philosophers, Socrates in partic-
ular, and reflects the uncertainties of a generation in which all
traditional religious and ethical beliefs were being challenged.

For this edition Alan Sommerstein has completely revised his
translation of the three plays, bringing out the full nuances of
Aristophanes' ribald humour and intricate word play, with a
new introduction explaining the historical and cultural back-
ground to the plays.

Translated with an introduction and notes by
ALAN H. SOMMERSTEIN

HOMER

The Iliad

'Look at me. I am the son of a great man. A goddess was my mother. Yet death and inexorable destiny are waiting for me'

One of the foremost achievements in Western literature, Homer's *Iliad* tells the story of the darkest episode in the Trojan War. At its centre is Achilles, the greatest warrior-champion of the Greeks, and his refusal to fight after being humiliated by his leader Agamemnon. But when the Trojan Hector kills Achilles' close friend Patroclus, he storms back into battle to take revenge – although he knows this will ensure his own early death. Interwoven with this tragic sequence of events are powerfully moving descriptions of the ebb and flow of battle, of the domestic world inside Troy's besieged city of Ilium and of the conflicts between the gods on Olympus as they argue over the fate of mortals.

E. V. Rieu's acclaimed translation of *The Iliad* was one of the first titles published in Penguin Classics, and now has classic status itself. For this edition, Rieu's text has been revised, and a new introduction and notes by Peter Jones complement the original introduction.

Translated by E. V. RIEU
Revised and updated by PETER JONES *with* D. C. H. RIEU
Edited with an introduction and notes by PETER JONES

HOMER

The Odyssey

*'I long to reach my home and see the day of my
return. It is my never-failing wish'*

The epic tale of Odysseus and his ten-year journey home after
the Trojan War forms one of the earliest and greatest works of
Western literature. Confronted by natural and supernatural
threats – shipwrecks, battles, monsters and the implacable
enmity of the sea-god Poseidon – Odysseus must test his bravery
and native cunning to the full if he is to reach his homeland
safely and overcome the obstacles that, even there, await him.

E. V. Rieu's translation of *The Odyssey* was the very first
Penguin Classic to be published, and has itself achieved classic
status. For this edition, Rieu's text has been sensitively revised
and a new introduction added to complement his original
introduction.

'One of the world's most vital tales ... *The Odyssey* **remains
central to literature'** MALCOLM BRADBURY

Translated by E. V. RIEU
Revised translation by D. C. H. RIEU
With an introduction by PETER JONES

VIRGIL

The Aeneid

'I sing of arms and of the man'

After a century of civil strife in Rome and Italy, Virgil wrote *The Aeneid* to honour the emperor Augustus by praising Aeneas – Augustus' legendary ancestor. As a patriotic epic imitating Homer, *The Aeneid* also provided Rome with a literature equal to that of Greece. It tells of Aeneas, survivor of the sack of Troy, and of his seven-year journey: to Carthage, falling tragically in love with Queen Dido; then to the underworld, in the company of the Sibyl of Cumae; and finally to Italy, where he founded Rome. It is a story of defeat and exile, of love and war, hailed by Tennyson as 'the stateliest measure ever moulded by the lips of man'.

David West's acclaimed prose translation is accompanied by his revised introduction and individual prefaces to the twelve books of *The Aeneid*.

'The most truthful translation ever, conveying as many nuances and whispers as are possible from the original' *The Times*

'Sweet prose, clear and clean and dancing like a mountain stream, as here . . . West opens the window and the winds bring life into Virgil's body' *Wall Street Journal*

Translated with an introduction by DAVID WEST

PLATO

The Last Days of Socrates

'Nothing can harm a good man either in life or after death'

The trial and condemnation of Socrates on charges of heresy and corrupting young minds is a defining moment in the history of classical Athens. In tracing these events through four dialogues, Plato also developed his own philosophy, based on Socrates' manifesto for a life guided by self-responsibility. *Euthyphro* finds Socrates outside the court-house, debating the nature of piety, while *The Apology* is his robust rebuttal of the charges of impiety and a defence of the philosopher's life. In the *Crito*, while awaiting execution in prison, Socrates counters the arguments of friends urging him to escape. Finally, in the *Phaedo*, he is shown calmly confident in the face of death, skilfully arguing the case for the immortality of the soul.

Hugh Tredennick's landmark 1954 translation has been revised by Harold Tarrant, reflecting changes in Platonic studies, with an introduction and expanded introductions to each of the four dialogues.

Translated by HUGH TREDENNICK *and* HAROLD TARRANT
With an introduction and notes by HAROLD TARRANT

THE STORY OF PENGUIN CLASSICS

Before 1946 ... 'Classics' are mainly the domain of academics and students; readable editions for everyone else are almost unheard of. This all changes when a little-known classicist, E. V. Rieu, presents Penguin founder Allen Lane with the translation of Homer's *Odyssey* that he has been working on in his spare time.

1946 Penguin Classics debuts with *The Odyssey*, which promptly sells three million copies. Suddenly, classics are no longer for the privileged few.

1950s Rieu, now series editor, turns to professional writers for the best modern, readable translations, including Dorothy L. Sayers's *Inferno* and Robert Graves's unexpurgated *Twelve Caesars*.

1960s The Classics are given the distinctive black covers that have remained a constant throughout the life of the series. Rieu retires in 1964, hailing the Penguin Classics list as 'the greatest educative force of the twentieth century.'

1970s A new generation of translators swells the Penguin Classics ranks, introducing readers of English to classics of world literature from more than twenty languages. The list grows to encompass more history, philosophy, science, religion and politics.

1980s The Penguin American Library launches with titles such as *Uncle Tom's Cabin*, and joins forces with Penguin Classics to provide the most comprehensive library of world literature available from any paperback publisher.

1990s The launch of Penguin Audiobooks brings the classics to a listening audience for the first time, and in 1999 the worldwide launch of the Penguin Classics website extends their reach to the global online community.

The 21st Century Penguin Classics are completely redesigned for the first time in nearly twenty years. This world-famous series now consists of more than 1300 titles, making the widest range of the best books ever written available to millions – and constantly redefining what makes a 'classic'.

The Odyssey continues ...

The best books ever written

PENGUIN 🐧 CLASSICS

SINCE 1946